The Jewish War of Survival

by
Arnold Spencer Leese

Historical Review Press
Surrey, England
2024

FIRST EDITION, SEPTEMBER, 1945

SECOND EDITION, APRIL, 1947

U. S. A. Copyright 194'7 By Arnold Leese

All Rights Reserved

Printed In the U. S. A.

for

Arnold Leese, 20, Pewley Hill, Guildford
Surrey, England

Reprinted 2024

Historical Review Press
3 Hillcroome Road, SM2 5EL
Online Bookshop: www.hrp.co.uk
E-mail: HRP@inbox.com
ISBN: 0-906879-24-8

Foreword

The first edition of my book took nine months to complete. I began work on it in the Spring of 1945. Berlin had fallen and Hitler had died among his soldiers. Mussolini had been bestially murdered. The San Francisco Conference was in full swing. The first edition of my book took nine months to complete. I began work on it in the Spring of 1945. Berlin had fallen and Hitler had died among his soldiers. Mussolini had been bestially murdered. The San Francisco Conference was in full swing.

This book has entailed many hundreds of hours of labour. Working entirely by hand, with the aid of a few friends, countless difficulties had to be overcome. Owing to the limited number of first edition copies produced, I asked my friends to make known the facts contained herein.

The appalling events which have taken place in Europe since the Spring of 1945 are sufficient justification for all that I have written. As long ago as 1924 I stated that there are two things worse, even, than war. The one is INJUSTICE. The other is a Bolshevist Peace!

ARNOLD LEESE
22nd December 1945

Dedicated to the hundreds of patriotic Britons who, with the Author, were imprisoned without charge or trial during the Second World War.

Preface

I stood, as Mr. Richard Stokes, M. P., stood for a negotiated peace, but, possibly, on vastly different grounds. Mr. Stokes was not interned, because he will not face the Jewish Menace. Since the beginning of the War, I did what little I could in favour of a negotiated peace, no matter which side was for the moment on top. I believe that the War was, from the National standpoint, a disaster-wrong and unnecessary. For holding similar views on other wars contemporary to them, such well known men as: Pitt, Fox, Bright, Lloyd George, RamsayMacDonald and the present Home Secretary Herbert Morrison were not interned. There is of course a difference in my case, as I am attacking the Jews and they were not, and the Jew holds supreme power.

I have attacked the Jews before and won a great moral victory over them. The Jews had me imprisoned for six months in 1936 for what was said to be a "public mischief" in that I mentioned in my paper, "The Fascist," the subject of Jewish Ritual Murder. Evidently judging me by their own standards, they thought to frighten me into silence. When I came out of prison I published a book on the subject, and they honoured me by maintaining a silence so intense that it could almost be heard! They were afraid to advertise it by taking another action against me. I defied them successfully and the book has since been distributed all over the world. I hope therefore to do it successfully again.

This War was Jewish and has never had any other object than the salvation of the Jews from Hitler. The first nine chapters of this book disprove the "causes" given from time to time by politicians and others for our being in a War which even the ignorant mob had sensed and labelled "phoney." The Tenth Chapter deals with a half truth prevalent amongst the better-informed. The rest of the book completes my case that the War was Jewish and that Britain was forced into it for Jewish purposes.

The World has only seen one more stupendous bluff than this war, and that was Jewish too.

ARNOLD LEESE
20 Pewley Hill,
Guildford, Surrey
5th May 1945

Preface to the. Second Edition

The first edition, limited a a few hundred copies produced by my friends after great exertion by the roneo process, was at once sold out.

In this second edition some changes have been made in the text and new material has been added. An index and Appendices have been included. Appendix I is on the War of Extermination which is still going on. Only the means have changed. Then it was bombing. Now it is starvation. Appendix IV is an outline of what the world rejected in Hitler's peace offer of April 1, 1936.

Appendix III is an unpublished letter on the Nuremberg Trial sent to the (London) Times. Appendix IV is on new appointments.

ARNOLD LEESE
1st April 1947

Contents

FOREWORD ..___ ..I
PREFACE 1st Edition ..___ ..III
PREFACE 2nd Edition . ..___ ..V
APPENDICES ..___ ..V
CHAPTER I We Fought to Save Poland's Independence .. ___..1
CHAPTER II "We Are Fighting In Defense of Freedom" (Lord Halifax) ___..9
CHAPTER III "We Are Fighting for Peace" (Lord Halifax) ..___..15
CHAPTER IV "We Are Meeting a Challenge to ur Own Security"
(Lord Halifax) . ..___..15
CHAPTER V "We Are Defending the Rights All Nations to Live Their
Own Lives" and "Fighting Against Substitution of Brute Force
for Law As the Arbiter Between Nations" (Lord Halifax) ..___..19
CHAPTER VI "We Are Fighting Against the Violation of the Sanctity
of Treaties and Disregard of the Pledged Word" ..___ ..25
CHAPTER VII "We Are Fighting Today for the Preservation of
Christian Principles" (The (London) Times, 17th Feb. 1940) ..___..27
CHAPTER VIII "We Are Fighting As Our Fathers Fought to Uphold
the Doctrine That All Men Are Equal In the Sight of God"
(Franklin D. Roosevelt, 6th Jan. 1942). ..___..33
CHAPTER IX "We Are Fighting for Democracy". ..___.. 37
CHAPTER X The Theory That High Finance Caused the War ..___..43
CHAPTER XI The Object Is to Destroy Fascism and Hitlerism. .,___..45
CHAPTER XII Unprepared and Blindfold ..___..49
CHAPTER XIII Hitler Always Knew His Real Enemy ..___..53
CHAPTER XIV Hitler Wanted Peace With Britain. .. ___..57
CHAPTER XV How Britain Was Egged On to Make War. ..___ ..61
CHAPTER XVI The Jews Acknowledge Their Power and threaten .. ___..67
CHAPTER XVII The Jews Declare War .. ___ ..71
CHAPTER XVIII The Jewish War ..___ ..79
CHAPTER XIX The Peace: Britain Defeated-Whoever Wins ..___..91
CHAPTER XX Conclusion ..___..95

Appendices

I The War of Extermination	97
II What the World Rejected: Hitler's Peace Offer of April 1, 1936	100
III The Nuremberg Trial..	101
IV New Appointments	103
Bibliography	106

Chapter I

WE FOUGHT TO SAVE POLAND'S INDEPENDENCE

Was it in defense of Poland that we were sent to War? Assurance of British support to Poland if she were attacked was officially announced by Prime Minister Neville Chamberlain on 31st March 1939 in these words:

"In the event of any action which clearly threatens Polish independence and which the Polish Government think necessary to oppose with their national forces, Britain and France will give all the support in their power." "In the event of any action which clearly threatens Polish independence and which the Polish Govevrnment think necessary to oppose with their national forces, Britain and France will give all the support in their power."

At first sight, it would seem that the independence of Poland was a cause upon which the British Empire was ready to stake its whole existence. A short contemplation of that theory is enough to dispose of it.

Poland's geographical position alone rendered it utterly impractical for us to protect that country's independence against the armed might of Germany. We may think what we like of the moral stature or moral 'dwarfdom' of the members of His Majesty's Government, but they are at least intelligent enough not to need to consult some twelve-year-old schoolgirl with her six-penny atlas in a matter so obvious. When they allowed Mr. Chamberlain to make this statement, almost but not quite unchallenged, they knew that success was impossible.

That is the point: They knew!

In other words, they acted without consideration for the welfare of their country and Empire in risking the annihilation of both for something they knew impossible to achieve. Lord Arnold condemned this pact with Poland as "... one of the most unwise decisions ever made by a British Government."

A few other members of the two Houses spoke in a similar strain, but that was all!

Within a month, the future slaughter was assured by the adoption of compulsory military training for all British males on reaching the age of twenty. The call for National Service had already been made in the form of a booklet sent to every household in the country and compiled by Humbert Wolfe, a Jew.

The formal agreement of Mutual Assistance was made on the 25th 1939 and was accompanied by a huge loan to Poland. Those who made it knew there could be no such thing as mutual assistance between Poland and Britain. By the time Britain could, by some miracle, operate to "save" Poland, the patient would be dead. Article 2 of this document left it to Poland to decide when the British Empire should risk all in war.

Our assistance was made to depend upon "action by a European Power which clearly threatened, directly or indirectly the independence" of Poland and "was of such a nature that the Party in question" (Poland) "considered it vital to resist with its armed forces." It was not left to Britain or France to do the considering. If the Polish Government considered, we had to come in. It is important, therefore, to recall that the Polish Foreign Minister at the time was Colonel Beck, son of a converted Jew, * and that the correspondent in England of the Polish Telegraph Agency was Stefan Litauer, also a Jew. Our Foreign Minister was Lord Halifax, whose son and heir married the grand-daughter of a Rothschild. Our War Minister was Hore-Belisha, a Jew.

When Col. Beck died in 1944, it was typical of the conspiracy of silence maintained by the Press, that the Times (London) obituary notice, although describing how Beck visited England to discuss the future agreement which dragged us into war, made no mention of him being a Jew.

"Polish Foreign Minister Joseph Beck is of Jewish origin," his father being "a converted Jew from Galicia." (Jewish Daily Post, 28th July, 1935.)

It might be suggested that we had heavy financial commitments and interests in Poland, and that the wicked capitalist was responsible for sending us to war to save his Polish bacon. But the capitalist knew just as well as the politicans that his capital in Poland could not be saved by any effort that Britain or France could make, but would on the outbreak of war run the risk of destruction with the certainty of confiscation by the enemy of any part of it escaping destruction.

Then, again, was this British capital in Poland important enough to preserve at the cost of war with Germany, even if it could have been saved thereby? A Jew, L. Welliscz, in his book FOREIGN CAPITAL IN POLAND gives figures showing that as late as 1937 less than 6 percent of foreign capital invested in Poland was "British, "27 per cent was "French," and 19 per cent was "United States." You are left to guess what proportion of this "British," "French" and "United States" capital was in fact Jewish, We know that the Prudential Assurance Company (whose Jewish connections are so powerful that it loaned half a million pounds to the Jewish town of Tel Aviv in Palestine in 1936 - a very shaky security) owned the Warsaw Prudential Assurance Company, which in turn, had big industrial 'interlockings' in Poland. But even from a soulless international capitalist's standpoint, between Germany and Poland, it was not for Poland that worth a war to preserve.

Although the war started as a result of the quarrel between Germany and Poland, it was not for Poland that Britain went to war. I have shown that Chamberlain's pledge and the agreement made later between Britain and Poland are inexplicable unless a non-British factor was the ruling influence. That non-British factor could only be the Jewish Money Power acting, this time, not in the interests of Jewish money alone but to make sure that Britain should throw her strength into a fight for the survival of the Jews.

Poland was a country in which Britain herself was not greatly interested. It was, however, a direct Jewish interest, just as Czechoslovakia was. Even the "Times" (London) admitted on the 4th April 1939 that:

"Jews are the chief owners of urban real estate in Poland."

Handbook No. 43, POLAND, published under the direction of the Historical Section of the Foreign Office, says:

"Society in Poland is badly balanced. In the country, all the power lay in the hands of the nobles; in the towns, in the hands of the Jews."

On the next page it says:

"Jewish control of trade and commerce so prejudiced these pursuits in the eyes of the Polish upper classes that they became practically a Jewish monopoly."

Poland was a sort of last refuge of the Jews and it was crowded with them. At the end of 1938, eleven big Jewish capitalists alone "worth" altogether 660 million zlothy or nearly 17 million pounds sterling at the pre war rate were operating in Poland. The Jewish Dr. Litauer wrote in QUERY in 1938 (quoted in Jewish Chronicle - London-March 24, 1944) that Jews constituted 62 per cent of those engaged in trade and commerce, and that only 23 per cent were workmen; whereas, even with out taking agriculture into consideration (a purely Gentile industry-A. L.) 53 per cent of the Gentiles in Poland were workmen and only 17 per cent were employers.

The above analysis of the situation shows that Poland was a Jewish interest rather than a British one. But I will go further and assert that not only was Poland not a British interest, but that Britain and the British Government do not care a straw about Poland. They have proved it both by their actions and by their inaction during the war itself.

When Germany was quickly over-running Poland in 1939 Russia stepped in, in the most literal sense of the term and occupied by force the Eastern half of that country. It was a pure act of aggression and caused the complete collapse of Polish resistance against Germany.

What was the reaction in Britain?

No one seemed to care very much.

German aggression was one thing - but Russian aggression was quite another.

Lloyd George, writing to the Polish Ambassador over here (London) said he was delighted that our Government has shown no indication of placing the Russian advance into Poland in the same category as that of the German!

It is, of course, easy to point out that to declare war on Russia because of her invasion of Poland would have been suicidal for the Allies. But can it be said to be any more suicidal than it was to declare war on Germany for doing the same thing? The alternative to declaring war on Russia for her aggression was to admit that nothing we could do would save Poland, and to make peace with Germany and withdraw from the war. But that would not have suited the Jews, so We continued the fight - which shows that it was not Poland we were worrying about.

Well, Russia was driven out of Poland by the Germans and after many days came back in 1943 and 1944. The old frontiers of Poland were again invaded by Russia. On the 18th October 1943, the "Times"

(London) in a leading article stated:
"Russia claims no extension of the frontiers held by her when Hitler unleashed his invading hordes in June, 1941; and after all that she has endured and achieved in the last two years, any proposal to curtail them would be clearly resented as ill-conceived and ill-timed."

No! There was nothing to be said for poor, weak Poland! It was a case of Russia's "liberating armies." It seems that the independence of Poland that we were supposed to have gone to war about really meant, at most, the independence of its Western half!

"... was satisfied that Mr. Eden would see that the Polish people were not overlooked in the redrawing of the map of Europe."

Surely this remark, after more than four years of frightful war "for the independence of Poland" deserves to be considered as a priceless pointer to the truth.

The Soviet's Jewish Ambassador to Mexico, Oumansky, was the first actually to drop a brick for his Government. He intimated in an address (according to the London Times, 12th Nov. 1943) that

"Russia regards as hers the Polish territory occupied in the summer of 1939."

Bagged! The Soviet Government confirmed this view in 1944.

A sham Government without mandate or country to rule over, was established for Poland in England. General Sikorski, its Premier, was provided with officers for his puppet Government by none other than Lord Nathaniel Rothschild, the friendship between the two, Gentile and Jew, being of long standing (Evening News, 18th Sept. 1942). Ah! These Rothschild chums!

Meanwhile in the real Poland which Russia had invaded, Polish Mayors and Town Councils had in many places been displaced by Jews, and here and there by Ukrainians. (London Times, 2nd Oct. 1939).

In 1943, the Germans stated that they had discovered a pit at Katin, near Smolensk, filled with the bodies of thousands of Polish officers who had been murdered they said, by the Russians. They had all been shot in the back of the head. The Polish puppet Government in London asked the International Red Cross to investigate the matter. The Soviet Government would not allow it and cancelled diplomatic relations.

Now, if Britain was so anxious in 1939 that the independence of Poland should be preserved at any price, is it not certain that the fate of many thousands of men of the best blood of Poland should be a matter of serious concern to her?

But, no!

Every method of damping down publicity for the frightful outrage was resorted to. The Germans were held accountable. Had the British Government really thought that this horrible record in mass-murder had been achieved by the Nazis, would it not have given the matter the utmost publicity? Neither the Polish nor the British authorities believed the story that these officers had been massacred by the Germans.

It leaked out that some ten thousand or more Polish officers captured by the Russians after the fighting of September, 1939, had been put into camps. Since early 1940 the Polish Red Cross had no news of them. The Russians say they were liberated but it is fairly certain they were liquidated.

The Soviets made their own investigation They blamed the Nazis for the murders. No one believed that. The British Government cared as little as though these finest of Poland's manhood had been stray cats. The situation was shamelessly summed up in the Daily Sketch with these words:

"It is recognized in diplomatic quarters that refusal to accept the testimonies of the Soviet Commission would finally close the door to Russo-Polish rapprochment." (27th January 1944.)

The British Government never insisted on an independent inquiry. The press was kept silent on the subject for a while and then democracy forgot all about it. *

The sham Polish Government had a lot of trouble about anti-Semitism in its army. This kept cropping up in incidents. Now that was something that the British Government could not overlook. It was not a matter of Polish officers being murdered. It was one of Jews being annoyed. That makes a difference. So the British Government prevented the Polish News (London Polish Weekly-Ed.) from continuing publication by withdrawing its paper supply. When the anti-semitism caused Jewish soldiers to desert, the sham Polish Government in London was informed officially of "the great importance which His Majesty's Government attached to the Polish Government's continuing and intensifying their efforts to eradicate any manifestations of anti-semitism in the Polish forces stationed in this country."

I have said enough to demonstrate that it never was Poles that the British Government was concerned about, but Jews. Murder ten thousand or more Polish officers and you can get away with it. Oppose the Jewish domination of your nation's affairs, or their participation in them, and if you are a Pole, the British Government will exert "pressure" on you. If you are a Briton, you will be put into Prison for years without charge or trial and the Courts will be used against you if you try, through them, to regain your liberty. Yes, even up to and including that ultimate Court of Appeal - the House of Lords itself.

So we did not go to war for Poland or the Poles. Mr. R. J. Davis, M.P., said in the House on 24th May 1944, that it is doubtful whether the British Government would have a word to say about the kind of Poland that... An article in the New Leader (D. S. A.) 14th October, 1943, page 5, by Alexander Kerensky, known among White Russian exiles as a half-Jew, Premier of the Provisional Government in Russia before the Bolshevik Revolution, reveals that General Sikorski knew for at least two years before the German discovery of the Katin pit of dead that these officers had disappeared but the General remained silent because of the effect that the mystery would have had on his Polish Army. would emerge after the conflict as "Stalin would determine that!" (He did-Ed.)

Russia will tolerate no border state that is not Bolshevised. The word "liberated" as applied to Poland is an odious and overworked hypocrisy. Churchill announced his submission to Stalin in these words:

"Territorial changes on the frontier of Poland there will have to be. Russia has a right to our support in this matter, because it is the Russian armies which alone can deliver Poland from German talons; and after all the Russian people have suffered at the hands of Germany, they are entitled to safe frontiers and to have a friendly neighbour on their Western flanks." (House of Commons, September 1944.)

Russia set up another Polish Government in Lublin and this Bolshevik Government was set up in Warsaw in 1945 without the consent of Britain. No protest was made by Britain. Thus the ostensible cause of our going to war is proved to be a sham. We were sent to war on false pretenses. That such a thing is possible illustrates the truth of my contention that Democracy is Death-in this case the death of Britannia that Ruled the Waves.

Chapter II

WE ARE FIGHTING IN DEFENSE OF FREEDOM"
Lord Halifax

Everyone is agreed that under Civilization there cannot be complete freedom. That is only obtainable under anarchy, with consequences few people would care to suffer. Therefore we may take it that Lord Halifax and others who say we are fighting for Freedom, mean Reasonable Freedom under civilized conditions. Freedom is divisible into (1) National Freedom, which is the subject dealt with in Chapter V, and (2) Personal Freedom, dealt with here.

Perhaps I have as good a right as any man to nail the lie that we fought this war in defense of Personal Freedom, since, for being actively anti-Jewish and for maintaining, like Mr. Richard Stokes, M. P., that it was better for everyone that the war would be brought to an early close by a negotiated peace rather than that it should be allowed to drag on, I was incarcerated in Brixton Prison three and one-quarter years (with a short interval of a few weeks in a dirty Concentration Camp) without being charged or tried for any offence, imaginary or otherwise. I was jailed so that I might not divulge to others the results of careful investigation into the menace of the Jew. But more of this anon.

For the last ten years the economic policy of the Government of this country has been mapped out for them by an organization called Political and Economic Planning, or P. E. P., for short. It was my paper THE FASCIST which first (July, 1933) gave publicity to the existence of this Jewish racket. Until then its existence was a carefully preserved secret. Israel Moses Sieff* and the first Lord Melchett, two wealthy Jews, were prominent in P. E. P.'s activities. A number of Gentile politicians were soon roped in P. E. P. is identical with the New Deal of the D. S. A.

Representative Louis T. McFadden, speaking in the House of Representatives (D. S. A.), 3rd May 1934, quoted Lord Melchett as saying, when asked by his fellow members of P. E. P. to show more activity in the organization:

"Let us go slowly for a while until we see how our Plan carries out in America."

The natural question is, "Whose plan?" The prominence of Jewish influence in the New Deal and in its English counterpart, P. E. P., leads inescapably to the answer:

The Jewish Plan of International Economic Control. The policy of P. E. P. is nothing less than the Sovietization of this country (Britain; of course. The reader knows of the New Deal parallel in America) by stealth.

Its whole trend is toward the dictatorship of Trusts and Combines; towards regimentation and standardization; and towards the elimination of the small trader and distributor. Those who have suffered from P. E. P.'s activities recognize it as a Planning Against Freedom.

P. E. P. has brought into being a number of Marketing Boards, the Electricity Grid, Import Duties Advisory Committee, the London Passenger Transport Board, Town and Country Planning Board, Committee on National Housing, International Congress for Scientific Management, Retail Trading Standard's Association, Federated Multiple Shop Proprietor's Association, and many others. None of these organizations is concerned with maintaining Personal Freedom, but with curtailing it.

The Rt. Hon. Walter Elliott was a member of the P. E. P. and Minister of Agriculture in 1936. In the words of Sir Arnold Wilson, M. P.:

"Every step he (Elliot) has taken has penalized the small farmer and the small retailer who finds him his market. He is not planning for employment, or for the increase in the number of those who may become their own masters... what he has done is to increase the market-value of shares in every distributing organization handling agriculture produce - the great aggregation of capital owned by anonymous shareholders, and directed by able and ambitious men who seek power for its own sake,"

Similar policies have been carried out in most departments of our national economic life. The policy of the Government, influenced by the Political Economic Planning ideas of centralization, has not been concerned with defence of Personal Freedom but with the increase of Jewish Control over economic life.

The economic policy of the Government, as announced in the White Paper of May 1944, indicates that restrictions and control are to continue long after the War is over. The object is not to promote freedom but to make life possible under a continuance of the practice of usury.

As recently as June 1944 a Bill was being forced through the Commons, against strong protests, to enable the Minister for Agriculture to ruin a dairy farmer if he thought that farmer was likely to transgress the law!

The spokesmen of the Government are fond of making speeches and writing articles to convey the false idea that Democracy (the sort represented by universal suffrage - the counting of heads regardless of contents, if any) is synonymous with Freedom. Actually, Democracy works out as the Dictatorship of Organized Money Power and that is a Dictatorship of the Jew.

The public was induced to believe that they fought for Freedom in this war. Are not the Allies, the British Empire, the U. S. A. and France democracies? As though modern democracy is any longer associated with Freedom. Soviet Russia has done most of the fighting on our side and China hangs on to our coat-tails. It is a grim joke to pretend that our Soviet ally is a democracy and not the dictatorship of a bandit controlled by the Jewish Money Power, or that the "common people" are the rulers! Neither Russia nor China has the faintest conception of Democracy or Freedom as the West understands these terms.

This Grand Alliance of Dictatorships and Democracies begins to take a recognizable shape when all the humbug about the association of Freedom with Democracy is cast side. Then it becomes clear that the Allied Powers are the Jewish Powers fighting for Jewry, indifferent as to whether they themselves are democracies or tyrannies and quite unconcerned with the ideal of personal freedom.

It is not disputed that freedom has to be curtailed in war-time. But there is this difference. In our past wars, when we were not under full Jewish control as we are now, individuals who disagreed with the supposed righteousness of their country's cause were allowed to say so publicly, so long as they did not actually interfere with the war itself. History records the following instances among many:

Pitt: who wrote and spoke against our cause in the American War of Independence.

Charles James Fox: who did the same in the Napoleonic Wars.

John Bright: who did the same in the Crimean War.

Lloyd George: who did the same in the Boer War.

Ramsay MacDonald: who did the same in the First World War.

Herbert Morrison: who did the same (I shall quote him elsewhere).

The Government which sent us to war with Germany in 1939 adopted a different code. It knew that its cause was so rotten, that it would not be able to stand public criticism, so it employed certain "Defense Regulations," notably that known as "Regulation 18B," against those men and women who knew too much about the real objects of our belligerency and were not afraid to say out aloud what they knew. These men and women were arrested and without charge or trial of any kind, flung into prison or camps and left there to rot for months and years.

(Tyler Kent, the American code clerk, was imprisoned for five years under 18B.-Ed.). * It did not matter that many of these people had served their country well in the last war. Their patriotism and past sacrifices counted for nothing. One Member of Parliament (Capt. A. H. M. Ramsay-Ed.), who had been shot in the heart during the last war, but had miraculously recovered, was imprisoned for over four years. British National Sentiment had caused the erection of War Memorials all over the country to men who had died from similar wounds. What mockery! "Memorials" !

But nothing was remembered. We were dispatched like sheep into a Second World War!

The Jewish Money Power, not National Sentiment, governed the situation in 1939.

Freedom? Freedom was sacrificed to save the Jew from criticism and exposure as the cause of the war.

Freedom of speech? No.

But freedom to say or write except what the Government called anti-semitism.

I was luckier than many. I had taken steps to avoid arrest as soon as I knew the Government's intentions regarding Freedom for the Jew-wise, When, human nature being what it is, through carelessness which so often betrays the successful fugitive, I was finally cornered and taken, enough time had elapsed for the "18B" inmates of prisons and camps to have secured passable conditions of life, hard as they were, especially in prisons. I did not have to endure the horrors of filth and solitary confinement for months, which others, no less patriotic than myself, had to undergo during the earlier part of their persecution.

I will not divert the reader's attention from the main issue by describing the horrors of the Jewish Democratic Ogpu in Britain. But I will say this: if any of my readers have any lingering idea that Democracy means .

Responsibility, then they must admit responsibility for vile outrages against patriotic but Jew-wise fellow Britons outrages of which the bestiality and sadism have not yet been allowed to become public knowledge. The details are well and truly described in IT MIGHT HAVE HAPPENED TO YOU, published by the Stickland Press, 104 George Street, Glasgow, C. 1 (Price 1/- plus 2d postage) - and don't forget it-it would have happened to you if, in the eyes of the Jewish Power, you had seemed hostile to it.

To cloak their object, the Government and its subservient Press spread widely the idea that the people interned under Regulation 18B were traitors or "Quislings" who preferred to see the Germans conquer Britain because they liked Germans better than Britons. The truth was that these men and women only wanted the War (which they knew to be Jewish) to be brought to a close by negotiation and the Jewish menace tackled vigorously by the British people themselves. They would no more relish the interference of Germany in the matter than that of any other foreign country.

Not only were Magna Carta, Habeas Corpus, and the Bill of Rights abandoned in the Jewish cause, but all Courts of Justice were used to deny to 18B litigants the very justice they were supposed to dispense. In the highest Court of Appeal, the House of Lords, decisions were made and judgments given which an honest dissentient Judge compared with those heard by Alice in the White Queen's Court in THROUGH THE LOOKING GLASS. To prevent 18B sufferers from obtaining relief, the House of Lords Judges decided that the words "If a man has" could be construed to mean "If a man thinks he has"! This ridiculous finding registers a low-water mark in the deterioration of "British Justice." It was only possible because of the desire to make "legal" the unconstitutional methods by which anti-Jewish patriots could be imprisoned for no offense. It is no accident that the case was taken to the House of Lords by a Jew. So if you are ever charged with a murder, all you have to do to establish an alibi is to swear that you think you were in Timbuctoo at the time of the crime, which, according to these precious Lords of Appeal, will count as evidence in your favour! Two, at least, of the four Lords of Appeal who gave the majority verdict have close family Jewish connections. How many were Freemasons, I do not know.

Therefore the Government has never been concerned with any concept of freedom at all and the number of members of Parliament who even took the trouble to raise their voices in protest against "18B" was distressingly small. In fact, many of them, perfectly aware that fellow countrymen were imprisoned for their political opinions without charge or trial, wrote or spoke as though no such thing existed as "18B." For example, Mr. A. V. Alexan der, First Lord of the Admiralty, said on 28th March 1943, "In the British Isles, in the Dominion, in the United States, no man need fear for his politics." At that time, I8B or some similar regulation, was at work in all the countries named by Mr. Alexander, to suppress the one truth that the War was Jewish.

As a result of the War - East Central Europe has been bolshevized. What this means is described by Kerensky in the New Leader, 16th October 1945: "It seems to be a general rule that the Communist dictatorship reduces to the position of hard labor convicts something between one-third and one-sixth of the population of any country in which it is installed ... 200,000 of the 'class enemy' ere deported from Lithuania after the Kremlin's liberation of that small country." King Peter of Yugoslavia said on 8th August 1945, " In my country there exists on a full scale the dictatorship of the Tito regime. Every trace of law has been wiped out from the State organization."

It is, therefore, clear that Freedom was not the ideal for which the Allies fought this war.

* 'The Case of Tyler Kent', by John Howland Snow.

Chapter III

"WE ARE FIGHTING FOR PEACE."
Lord Halifax.

Well, we heard that one before. The last war was to be a War to end Wars.
If we are fighting for peace, why declare war?
The nonsensical statement which heads this Chapter is the typical humbug of the typical "democratic states man." It is without meaning, self-contradictory and merits no argument.

Chapter IV

"WE ARE MEETING A CHALLENGE TO OUR OWN SECURITY"
Lord Halifax

Coupled with this argument is the idea expressed by the words: "We had to stop Hitler!" an idea more widely believed in than any other of the false reasons upheld as causes of the War. The supposed necessity for action to equalize the Balance of Power in Europe is another facet of the self-defence theory.
Hitler and his Germany were getting so strong that we could not afford to let him get any stronger - we must fight to stop them. That was the argument. Those who upheld it as the correct one must show that Britain was threatened by Germany's new strength and by the increase of that strength which would result from her over powering attack on Poland.
Talkative " statesmen" have unconsciously knocked the bottom out of this argument. Mr. Joseph E. Davies, United States Ambassador to the Soviet Union from 1936 to 1938 and to Belgium in 1939, is one of these. He is entitled to be regarded as intelligent because he foresaw what so many did not - the potential strength of the Soviet Armies. He also realized the military strength of the Nazis. But he gave the game completely away in reporting to Acting Secretary of State, the Hon. Sumner Welles, in a letter dated 22nd August 1939 in which he wrote: "It was perfectly clear that if Europe were to have peace, it would have

to be a Fascist peace imposed by the dictators unless England and France created a countervailing East-and-West Axis by the inclusion of the Soviets, and established a balance of power which would keep peace through an equilibrium of forces ... The peace of Europe, if maintained, is in imminent danger of being a peace imposed by the dictators, under which all the small countries will speedily rush to get under the shield of the German aegis ..."

Here Mr. Davies admits, and officially advises his Chief, that PEACE WAS POSSIBLE. The conditions of that peace was that Continental Europe would be led by Hitler's Germany. It is therefore admitted that what is know as the "military menace of the Nazis" need not result in war.

Obviously, therefore, when Britain went to war "about Poland," it was not because she was threatened herself, but because the power behind the Government wanted at all costs to prevent Hitler's Germany from leading Continental Europe.

Lord Croft, Joint Parliamentary Secretary to the War Office, speaking at the Constitutional Club on 28th October 1942 said:

"We can claim that in an imperfect world, our faith and actions are less materialistic than in most countries, for we alone went into this conflict without being attacked; we of the British Empire drew the sword for the right of small nations to live."

No question here of danger to Britain. Lord Croft rejoices in the idea that we went to war "to save others"!

Sir Walter Elliot (M. P.) announced at the Albert Hall at the end of October, 1942, that he "considered that the atrocities of the Nazis were, more than any other single factor, the cause of Great Britain going to war" (reported in London Jewish Chronicle, 6th November 1942). This Privy Counsellor gave no impression of our having been threatened by Germany. We must refer again to Joseph E. Davies for the concrete proof that Britain was not the German objective. He closed on 20th January 1943 that the Germans in 1940 offered to retire Hitler if by so doing they could make peace with Britain. The condition attached to this offer was that Germany should be allowed to maintain its dominant position in Europe. Mr. Davies made this disclosure at a Town Hall meeting in Los Angeles, says the (London) Times of 22nd January 1943.

It is plain that Britain was never threatened. Therefore, in assessing the degree of aggression of which the various warring States are guilty, the most flagrant is surely Britain's. She could not bear to see another State getting stronger!

And they tell us we went to war to prevent aggression! No wonder people called this war "phoney."

Chapter V

"We are defending the rights of all Nations to live their own lives" and fighting against the substitution of brute force for Law as the arbiter between Nations."

Lord Halifax.

Our actions and those of our Allies during the War indicate that no nation will be allowed to live its own life if that life, in the way the nation concerned wants to live it, either (1) endangers our vital interests, or (2) excites the greed of our American and Soviet Allies. In composing the above statement of the case as I see it, I have given Britain credit for a less aggressive attitude towards small nations than the Allies seem to me to have shown.
Let us examine our own actions.
As soon as it seemed advisable from the standpoint of our own safety, we took over Iceland as a temporary measure against the will of the Icelandic people who were independent under the Kingship of the King of Denmark. The people of Iceland did not want to be dragged into the arena of war. Their actions toward the occupying troops, both British and American, testified to that.
It will be said that we went into Iceland to get there before the Germans. That makes no difference to the falsity of the argument that we are fighting to defend the right of Iceland to live its own life in its Own way. The Icelanders did not want us and they showed it in their behavior towards the invaders.
Senator Chandler of Kentucky, speaking on "a course of national action which would have the support of certain elements in the United States which have great power" (in the opinion of the 'Times' correspondent) advocated that the U. S. A. should keep the strategic bases "so painfully acquired" in Iceland and the French - owned New Caledonia.' (London Times, 8th October 1943.)
On August 25th, 1941, Britain in concert with Soviet Russia invaded Iran (Persia) against native resistance which collapsed on 9th September. The Shah, as a result, was forced to abdicate within a week. In this case,

not only did we allow Bolshevism to overrun Persia, but we forced its ruler off his throne because we didn't like him. We cared nothing for the idea of letting the Persians live their own lives. It is doubtful now whether they will ever again have a chance to live any other life than Bolshevik one.

The Portuguese press has been very outspoken in sarcastic criticism of all this talk about the rights of small nations. The small nations, it seemed, were becoming more and more docile satellites and victims of the Great Powers. The paper 'Seculo' said the Atlantic Charter has been smothered by Moscow. 'Vox' protested against economic restrictions which were forced upon neutrals in defiance of their rights to sell their goods as they wished (that is: to live their own lives). It criticized the threats made in the United States press against Argentina and suggested that the New York press assumed the Atlantic Charter was obsolete. The only bright spot, it said, is in the fact that all this violence against small nations is not backed up by actual bombardment!

Mr. Summer Welles, Under-Secretary of State of the United States in September 1941, has revealed that Britain was then planning to invade and occupy the Canary Islands at the risk of war with Spain.' It is also known that President Roosevelt ordered Admiral Stark to prepare a force to seize the Azores from Portugal, but the order was cancelled.

Mr. Duff Cooper, one our three leading war-mongers, was quite unconscious of any desire to allow small nations to "live their own lives." Writing in the 'Daily Mail' of 12th April 1940 he declared:

"We must not ask questions as to what these small powers want, nor listen to explanations of what they are prepared to do. Having made plain to them that it is their freedom and independence that are at stake, we must tell them frankly what we demand, what part each of them has got to play in the alliance that is to destroy the German menace. If one or the other of them shows signs of hesitation, we must act so as to insure that such hesitations will be immediately overcome. It is time similar measures were taken with regard to Holland and Belgium.

Be it remembered that Mr. Duff Cooper was a Privy Counsellor! He was not worrying about small nations living their own lives, but coercing them to do what he wanted them to do so that they might emerge Democratic and Jewish. And Mr. Duff Cooper has lately been chosen to be our Ambassador at Paris!

The Allies forced Spain in 1944 to curtail her trade in wolfram with Germany and to take action hostile to German interests. This was done by starving Spain of petrol.

Portugal was "induced" to allow the Allies to use the Azores as a flying base by similar measures.

The Earl of Selbourne, Minister for Economic Warfare, in the House of Lords on 3rd May 1944 voiced the distorted view of his government on neutrality thus:

"There was a heavy responsibility on all neutral Governments who valued independence and liberty to see that no act of theirs should assist those evil forces whose triumph would obliterate liberty from the world." This dictim, of course, assumes that all neutrals think the same about Germany (and Russia!) as Lord Selborne does. But it happens that Spain, Portugal, and Argentina took an opposite view to that of Lord Selbourne. They refer Germany to the Jewish Money Power. When one recalls how Persia was treated by the Allies, Lord Selbourne's speech seems disgusting enough.

Eire has had her experiences too. Treated with extraordinary and suicidal leniency long before the war when the game was to weaken Britain by depriving her of the Naval Bases on the West Coast, she must have been surprised to receive a demand from the United States to get rid of the representatives of Germany whom Ireland, as a neutral, allowed to function in Dublin. Surely this demand was an interference of considerable magnitude with Eire's "living her own life," seeing that it would, had she not rebuffed the proposal, have converted her from a neutral into an enemy of Germany.

The United States, by a formal statement of President Roosevelt, * had also condemned the suppression of Jewish newspapers in the Argentine. This is another example of bullying pressure upon a neutral state.

And what of our ally, Soviet Russia? When her interests were at stake, she invaded Poland and kept its Eastern half as long as she could until the Germans pushed her out of it. Then, when Russia in her turn pushed the Germans back into Poland, she allowed her spokesmen to announce that she regarded the territory she took in September, 1939, as her own! On the 3rd of August, 1939, Russia "incorporated Lithuania into the Soviet Union. Two days later, Latvia and on the next day Esthonia. All this before we adopted her as our "glorious ally." Thus, we knew perfectly well that this ally was quite indifferent to the supposed right of weak nations "to live their own lives." The three states were allowed to disappear with hardly a murmur.

When Russia reoccupied Lithuania, Latvia and Esthonia later in the war, her allies, who are supposed to have gone to war to preserve the independence and liberties of small nations, maintained an ominous silence.

On 30th November 1939 Soviet Russia had attacked Finland. In 1941 the Soviets became our Ally, but not for the purpose of "defending the rights of small nations to live their own lives."

Can anyone, except an Archbishop, really believe that there has been a sudden change of heart in Russia which will lead her to tolerate the independent existence of her weak neighbors? If anyone does, let him read what the owner of that grand old Russian name Yerusalemnsky wrote in the 'Red Star' early in 1944. Professor Yerusalemsky, referring to a proposal which had been voiced that the smaller Powers should confer together to protect their own interests, stated:

"How can one imagine Czechoslovakia, the victim of Hungary, and Yugoslavia, the victim of Bulgaria, meeting for such a purpose? Only the great democratic powers, war has shown, can form a stronghold against aggression; and only they can make peace secure."

Unquestionably this Jewish professor speaks for the Jewish influenced Soviet regime.

A speech of Molotov at the Sixth Session of the U. S. S. R. Supreme Soviet on 29th March 1940, when he was Chairman of the Council of Peoples' Commissars for Foreign Affairs, shows conclusively that this responsible official did not believe in the British talk about the "rights of small nations." He declared:

"Germany had become a dangerous competitor for the principal Imperialist Powers of Europe, Great Britain and France. They therefore declared war on Germany under the pretext of fulfilling their obligations to Poland. It is now clearer than ever how far the real aims of the Governments of these Powers are from the purpose of defending disintegrated Poland or Czechoslovakia. This is shown if only by the

fact that the Governments of Great Britain and France have proclaimed that their aim in this War is to smash and dismember Germany, although this is still being concealed from the mass of the people under cover of slogans of defending 'democratic' countries and the 'rights of small nations.' "
(Moscow News, 1st April 1940)

It is known further that the Peace Treaties to be forced upon the vanquished enemies are to contain a clause preventing discrimination and restrictions on racial grounds, thus, interfering with any possibility of these nations "living their own lives" (subsequently confirmed. -Ed.).

Meanwhile, the United States will continue to live its own life and discriminate, and rightly, against the Negro in its midst.

Lastly, the San Francisco Conference decided that Might is Right after all-the Big Powers would speak the final word in international disputes.

So much for the idea of "substituting law for brute force."

What the San Francisco Conference did was to legalize brute-force.

*The Washington, D. C., Star published (February 29th, 1936) a genealogy of President Roosevelt's family prepared by the Carnegie Institute of Washington, D. C. The Jewish descent of the first Roosevelts who emigrated from Holland to America is indicated.

"Roosevelt had a tinge of Jewish blood in him, for the first Roosevelt who came to New Amsterdam in 1649 married a Miss Jeanette Samuel." (Rabbi Louis G. Reynolds writing in the California Jewish Voice, April 20, 1945.) They affected complete indifference about the fate which befell them!

Chapter VI

"We are fighting against the violation of the Sanctity of Treaties and disregard of the Pledged Word."
Lord Halifax

This "cause of the war" is no cause at all.
It assumes that Germany is the only country whose rulers break Treaties. It leaves out of account the many changes of circumstances in international politics which make it impossible always to act according to Treaty when the conditions under which the Treaty was made have completely changed.
In no case affecting the collapse of Treaties involving Germany and Great Britain were Britain's interests vitally affected.
Britain was never elected as the International Policeman of the World. But Britain was drafted as a Special Constable by the Jewish Money Power to "stop Hitler."
It must be remembered that Germany has always held that the Versailles Treaty had been broken by Allied Powers. Germany was disarmed in order to establish a basis for general disarmament. But no parallel degree of disarmament was adopted by the other Powers who signed the Treaty. On this Hitler based much of his foreign policy. Germany, defenceless and ringed by power fully armed neighbors. What Government could remain inactive in the face of such a provocative situation and justify itself before its people?
Britain has a better record than any other country in the world for sticking to her treaties' terms; but the fact that she willingly allied herself with Russia proves that it was not Breaking of Treaties that she regarded as justifying war. Was not Soviet Russia expelled from the League of Nations for breaking her obligations under the Covenant by a treacherous and unprovoked attack on Finland in 1939? Does not the London Times Review of the Year 1940 declare that Russia tried to subdue Finland "with savage disregard for the rules of war"?
As for the Pledged Word apart from Treaties, the less the Allies preach of this, the better. In 1915, Sir Henry MacMahon, the High Commissioner

for Egypt (who was a 33rd degree Mason of the International Scottish Rite), promised in the name of Britain that in return for Arab assistance to the Allies, Great Britain would recognize and support the independence of the Arabs in territories which included Palestine. Two years later, our politicians traded away Palestine to the Jews as the only possible means of getting the United States into the First World War against Germany. (See p. 69.) It would be hard to find a worse case of treachery and breaking of the Pledge Word than this. No doubt because it was perpetrated for the sake of Jewry, it goes comparatively unnoticed. But the "treachery and aggression" of Hitler-that is headlined by the subservient press the world over.

Before leaving Munich on his peace mission in September, 1938, Neville Chamberlain signed with Hitler a declaration pledging their two countries to seek peaceful means of settlement of any future difference arising between them. Within a year, however, the British Government made its agreement with Poland whereby they handed over to that country the initiative for making war between Britain and Germany.

Our Declaration of War against Germany was not made in righteous indignation against "treachery" or "violation of the Sanctity of Treaties and disregard of the Pledged Word." We went to war with Germany without clean hands ourselves. Later we accepted as Allies the breakers of treaties, glad that they should pull us out of the mess into which we had allowed our politicians to plunge us. We finished by tearing up our treaty with Poland and abandoning her to the Bolsheviks.

Chapter VII

"We are fighting today for the preservation of Christian Principles."
A Leading Article, London Times, 17th February 1940

So have said many public men of the Allied Nations.
The lie is obvious enough. China is not Christian and does not want to be. Professor Chau, who held the post, in Australia, of Director of Information for the Chinese Ministry, reminded us of this in 1944. The press reports indicate that he made it clear that he distrusted the West which, he said, came to the East "with a gun in one hand and a Bible in the other."
Millions of Mohammedans are involved in the results of this war and thousands of them are fighting in it. Some Hindus are in it, too. None of the people care a fig for "Christian Principles."
But again, it is our Ally, Soviet Russia that affords us the easiest way of nailing this impudent lie. Not only is Soviet Russia non-Christian, but it is so hostile to it that a special Government Department has been maintained, staffed for the most part with Jews, for anti-God propaganda. In 1930, the Church of England officially denounced the persecution of Christians in Russia. The Archbishop of Canterbury (Dr. Lang) declared: ".... it was almost unparalleled in the pitiful history of religious persecution" and that "the persecution has been accompanied by popular blasphemies and obscenities.'
Lately, the easy consciences of priests and others have been satisfied by another pronouncement of the same Archbishop. He conveniently discovered that:
"The Soviet Government had abandoned some of the mistakes of its earlier regime" and that "criticisms of the past were now irrelevant in view of the issues at stake," and "there were some features in Russian Communism which were compatible with the Christian spirit." (House of Lords, 23rd October 1941.)
In view of the above it must be recalled that the London Jewish Chronicle announced that (4th April, 1919) :
" ... there is much in the fact of Bolshevism itself, in the fact that

So many Jews are Bolshevists, in the fact that the ideals of Bolshevism at many points are consonant with the finest ideals of Judaism."

It cannot to often be repeated that in Russia there is no Communism and there never has been any. They have a State of Capitalism run by Jews. Communism is the idea by which the ignorant masses are induced to accept Bolshevism. Communism remains an idea but it is never practiced.

The present Archbishop of York (Dr. Garbett) visited Russia in 1943-his tour comprised one city only. He came back to report what he went out to report. There is no need to stress it. He fell into line just as he did in the matter of bombing civilians in war. But I doubt if any of the clergy believed him.

Did the Pope do any better?

According to the Lisbon correspondent of the London Times, 22nd April 1943:

"He is known to have communicated verbally to the episcopate throughout the world that while Nazi doctrines were wholly inimical to Christianity, that the Communist, * evil as it was, could be regarded as in some sense a corruption of part of the Christian ethic."

Could anything be more pitiful than that?

Not one of the priests spoke the truth that Bolshevism-is Jewish, hence its "blasphemies and obscenities." It would be interesting to know what influence Freemasonry has had in these convenient changes of heart in high religious circles.

NOTE

"The Vatican considers the spread of communism in Europe, as the consequence of a Russian victory, to be less of a danger than nazism.
-Camille Cianfarra, N. Y. Times Magazine, Oct 4 1942).

The last thing the people who made the war cared about was Christianity. But as a weapon in propaganda they spread the story that Christianity was being persecuted in Germany. However, the Bishop of Gloucester visited Germany in 1938 and in a half column letter to the London Times, 14th July that year, he revealed the untruth of this propaganda. He said:

"German pastors of different schools of thought are (as far as he could judge-Ed.) free to carry on their work, provided they do not use their pulpits for political purposes. Pastor Neimoller is in confinement because he has stubbornly and determinedly defied this law."

Many times during the war, Christians have been startled to hear of happenings which did not seem to tally with Christian conduct of it, making every allowance for the excesses which are liable to occur in any war as the result of excitement and temporary loss of self-control. One instance was the bombing of cities.

It was the "non-Christian" Hitler who proposed on March 31, 1936, that incendiary bombs should be prohibited and that no bombs of any kind should be dropped on open towns outside the range of medium-heavy artillery.

But it was the "Christian Powers" who rejected the proposal.*

Another was the discovery of a pamphlet on Guerrilla Warfare published by the members of t he Staff of the (British) War Office (No. 1. Osterly Park), in which the text recommended the questioning of prisoners to induce them to give information before killing them.

Edgar L. Jones, an American, who served for over a year with the British Eighth Army in North Africa, and served as the Atlantic Monthly (Boston, Mass., U. S. A.) correspondent in the Far Pacific, writes his impression of the war in the February, 1946, number of the Atlantic Monthly:

"We Americans have the dangerous tendency in our international thinking to take a holier-than-thou attitude toward other nations. We consider ourselves to be more noble and decent than other peoples, and consequently in a better position to decide what is right and wrong in the world. What kind of war do civilians suppose we fought, anyway? We shot prisoners in cold blood, wiped out hospital, strafed lifeboats, killed or mistreated enemy civilians, finished off the enemy wounded, tossed the dying into a hole with the dead, and in the Pacific boiled the flesh off enemy skulls to make table ornaments for sweethearts, or carved their bones into letter openers. We topped off our saturation bombing and burning of enemy civilians by dropping atomic bombs on two nearly defenseless cities, thereby setting an all-time record for instantaneous mass slaughter.

"As victors we are privileged to try our defeated opponents for their crimes against humanity; but we should be realistic enough to appreciate that if we were on trial for breaking international laws, we should be found guilty on a dozen counts. We fought a dishonorable war, because morality had a low priority in battle....

"Not every American soldier, or even one per cent of our troops, deliberately committed unwarranted atrocities and the same might be said for the Germans and Japanese. The exigencies of war necessitated many so called crimes, and the bulk of the rest could be blamed on the mental distortion which war produced. But we publicized every inhuman act of our opponents and censored any recognition of our own moral frailty in moments of desperation.

"1 have asked fighting men, for instance, why they- or actually, why we - regulated flame-throwers in such a way that enemy soldiers were set afire, to die slowly and painfully, rather than be killed outright with a full blast of burning oil. Was it because they hated the enemy so thoroughly? The answer was invariably, 'No, we don't hate those poor bastards particularly; we just hate the whole goddam mess and have to take it out on somebody.' Possibly for the same reason, we mutilated the bodies of enemy dead, cutting off their ears and kicking out their gold teeth for souvenirs, and buried them with their testicles in their mouths, but such flagrant violations of all moral codes reach into still unexplored realms of battle psychology." (One War Is Enough.)

Edgar Jones is not alone in telling how this war "for the preservation of Christian Principles" was fought. Frank Coniff, of the New York Journal-American, writes in his column, East Side, West Side, of a conversation with Holbrook Bradley, another correspondent who "took off" in a tank, who told me it was a common custom to solve the prisoner problem by the most direct means.

"The tankers, sheathed in their iron horses, were unable to drag PWs back to the rear cages. They had to do something with them. So they did.

"They machine-gunned them to death. And made no apology for it.

"Combat veterans aware of the real situation know I am only scraping the surfaces. Rumors were always rife of mass liquidations of German PWs, especially by our tankers." (23rd May 1946.)

Then there is the message of the U. S. A. General Mark Clark to the Fifth Army on 12th February 1944 in which he said he welcomed the enemy's assaults:

"... for it gives you additional opportunities to kill your hated enemy in large numbers. It is an open season in Anzio beachhead and there is no limit to the number of Germans you can kill."

With what disgust must British and American officers and soldiers have received this talk about "the hated enemy."

Dr. Alington, Bishop of Durham, in his book The LAST CRUSADE, asks himself:

"What, for a Christian, are the conditions of a righteous war?" and gives the answer,

"One from which hate is as far as possible banished.'

Of the British press, it was the Sunday papers which were the chief hate propagandists. Perhaps my readers may recollect the Sunday Chronicle's article of 12th October 1941 by W. J. Brittain: "If Huns Came to Britain" or the article in the Sunday Express of 29th August 1943 headed "This is Your Good, Kind German." It was so full of hate that the author remained anonymous.

Actually this war has done more harm to Christianity than anything its virulent enemies could possibly have devised against it. People are not going to forget the bombings and other horrors (including I8B) and the attitude of high dignitaries of the Churches towards them. Nor will they forget the phosphorous grenades used by the U. S. A. troops and the flame-throwers. Presumably Christians sanctioned them.

The following sentences are quoted from the American Magazine Life:

"The shower of molten burning particles that sprays from a phosphorous shell sears its victims with agonizing burns. Used against pill-boxes the flame not only burns occupants but also suffocates them." (19th June 1944.)

Not a word from the Archbishops about that! It was not Christianity we fought for, but Judaism and Jewish revenge.

*Refer to Appendix II, page 100.

Chapter VIII

"We are fighting as our fathers fought to uphold the doctrine that all men are equal in the sight of God."
Franklin D. Roosevelt, 6th January 1942

These words were spoken by the President of the United States in a message to Congress. He continued:
"... We must be particularly vigilant against racial discrimination in any of its ugly forms."
If all men are equal in the sight of God, it would seem to be of little use for man here below to fight about it. Any decision about it will certainly be settled over his head.
But not all men think, as President Roosevelt would like them to think, that God regards men so. Anyhow with the senses God has provided him, sight, smell, hearing, touch, and taste. Ordinary Man certainly does not believe that all men are equal. President Roosevelt's fellow-countrymen don't for they discriminate against the Negro in their midst.
In June, 1944, in Ohio, a strike took place holding up 12,000 men on aeroplane construction because seven Negroes had been employed on work usually done by white men. The Southern States prohibit intermarriage between white and black, and enforce separate travel accommodations.
We British also, and in my opinion rightly, discriminate between ourselves and the coloured population of the Empire. In S. W. Africa, a proclamation, No. 19 of the 18th July 1934, makes extra-marital sexual intercourse between Europeans and Africans punishable with five years penal servitude or expulsion from the country. Col. D. Reitz, High Commissioner for the Union of South Africa, spoke at the London Guildhall on the 13th March 1944 insisting on the actual inequality of white and black in his country. Before the white man came to South Africa, he said, it lay uninhabited save for a few wandering Hottentots and Bushmen. The cities, ports, railways, roads and bridges and the civilization of South Africa were the White Man's creation. Every European would agree, he said, that to confer complex civil

rights upon a people who, as yet, were incapable of exercising them, would spell disaster. (Col. Reitz was too close to his subject to have observed that disaster has come to England itself from that very cause!)

The Jews themselves don't believe in Human Equality, any more than they believe in Communism. Both are ideas which they have successfully used in the degradation of the White Man's civilization. Jews have a number of uncomplimentary words expressing the inferiority of the Gentiles among whom they live. One such word is Goyim, meaning cattle. That this word is in actual use we quote from the Jewish Post, 7th December 1945, from the column - The Yiddish Press by Rabbi Benjamin Schultz:

"It's about time, comments the DAY'S - S. Nigor, to stop paying the expenses of goyim from Washington, because they express sympathy with the Jews. They come and read speeches at banquets, these big-shots. 'Read' - because we have written the speeches for them. But why waste more time and money? Now we want action. Words are cheap."

There can be no greater absurdity and no greater disservice to humanity in general than to insist that all men are equal. The idea is particularly favored by people with an inferiority complex. This can be traced to actual racial inferiority. It plays a double role; first, inducing people to tolerate doctrines dangerous to their society; and second, to permit finally their society to be dominated by these doctrines.

In a discussion, MARXISM AND JUDAISM by Saluste, the Jewish origin of the doctrine of equality is set forth in detail in a long quotation from ANTI-SEMITISM, ITS HISTORY AND CAUSES (Paris, Leon Chailley, 1894), by Bernard Lazare, great Israelite scholar of high moral probity:

"... The Jews believed not only that Justice, Liberty and Equality could become sovereign on this earth, but they held themselves (as) singled out especially to work for such sovereignty. All desires, all the hopes that these ideas gave birth to, ended by crystallizing around one central idea: that of the times of the Messiahs, of the coming of the Messiah."

The Chosen People idea, a people especially singled out by God, gives the Jews a stronger interest than any other people in establishing racial tolerance in a Christian society while at the same time maintaining their Own racial exclusiveness.

Thomas Jefferson in his Declaration of Independence wrote, "We hold these truths to be self-evident, that all men are created equal. ..." On such a shaky foundation arose the United States of America with Negro slavery in full blast in the South.

Perhaps the subject can best be disposed of by quoting at some length the thoughts of a great English Divine on the subjects of Race and Inequality. Dr. Arnold Ruby wrote as follows on 22nd March 1835 to the Archbishop of Dublin:

"With regard to such races as have been found in a savage state, if it be admitted that all mankind are originally one race, then I should say they must have degenerated; but if the physiological question be not settled yet, and that there is any reason to suppose that the New Hollander and the Greek never had one common ancestor, then you would have races of mankind divided into those improvable by themselves, and those improvable by others.' In a letter to W. W. Hull, dated 27th April 1836, Dr. Arnold wrote:

"The Jews are strangers in England and have no more claim to legislate for it than a lodger has to share with the landlord in the management of his house. If we had brought them here by violence, and then kept them in an inferior condition, they would have had just cause for complaint; though even then I think we might ... remove them to a land where they might live by themselves independent; for England is a land of Englishmen, not of Jews." (Page 402.)

These wise words, written before the works of Darwin, deserve to be better known. They have been taken from Dean Stanley's LIFE OF ARNOLD.

James Theophile Meek, noted archaeologist, has some thing to say about the origin of the Jews which may account for their feeling of inferiority:

" ... Wherever used 'Habiru' is a term of reproach, and just so its equivalent in Hebrew, ' ibri' is, a degrading, derogatory appellation, a mark of inferiority, denoting an alien, a barbarian, a Bedouin, a mock name that ridiculed its bearers'" (Hebrew Origins, page 9.) *

Even the London Times of 3rd July 1943 has been driven by the absurdity of the position to print:

"Frankly to recognize this divine law of inequalities seems specially important in these days."

Yes, but a little belated if, as Roosevelt says, we are in a World War to uphold the very opposite!

In his article Marxism and Judaism, Salluste makes a masterful analysis of the cult of equality beginning with Moses Mendelssohn, through Leopold Zunz, Heinrich Heine to Karl Marx, all adherents of what he has termed neo-Messianism. The path leads through Liberalism, Socialism, the negation of the Christian State, to atheistic Bolshevism inspired by Jewish neo-Messianic intellectuals, to civil war and, we may add, finally to World War.

*American Journal of Semitic Languages, XLIX, page 298.

Chapter IX

"WE ARE FIGHTING FOR DEMOCRACY"
A common catch phrase.

I ask my readers to look upon this proposition, that we are fighting for Democracy, on its own merits apart from questions of aggression, etc.
The Democracy which was established in units of the British Empire and in France, Belgium and the U. S. A., is the represented by the counting of heads. The majority is then able to put what are called its "representatives" in power. This is supposed to result in a government of the People, by the People, and for the People. But it is no such thing. The people lose all control over its "representatives" as soon as the latter come into office, for then they do what they like with the People. They can send them to War and Death, they can Ally them with Bolsheviks, they can offer (as Churchill, did, like an hysterical old woman) common citizenship with Nations of entirely different temperament and outlook on life. They can imprison them for years without charge or trial, as they did to me, and might have done to you. If the reader has left a vestige of the idea that Democracy means the responsibility of the people for the acts of the Executive. perhaps he will send me a cheque for his share in the responsibility for this disgusting outrage.
No, Democracy is a fraud!
By means of Democracy, however, the people can, for the most part, be taught to believe what they are told. If the people reads its newspapers and magazines, listen to its wireless (radio), gapes at its cinemas, absorbs the speeches of its politicians, believing all the time that these are all bonafide and British, when actually they are influenced by the alien ideas, largely masonic and Jewish.
The People constantly exposed to these influences will not think like Britons but like Jews, and now, for the most part, do. Karl Marx, great Jewish logician and penetrating thinker that he was, wrote in what is known as "Requisitore a la Drumont":
" ... and the practical Jewish spirit has become the spirit in practice of the Christian people. The Jews have been emancipated in (precise)

measure as the Christians have become Jews." (1844.)

If there is any independent thought left among the People there are drugs, particularly Spirits and Tobacco, to lull them into bovine complacency and finally the doctrines of freemasonry to keep a more definite hold upon them.

This is why these alien influences are so keen to get the people to believe that Democracy means Freedom. Given the Universal Vote, or something near it, these alien influences can control all the machines that manufacture what is called "public opinion." This control depends ultimately on the use of overwhelming Money Power. Quoting Karl Marx from the first part of the paragraph quoted above.

"The Jew has been emancipated, not only by making himself master of the financial market and because, thanks to him and by him, gold has become a world power ..."

It is not that these influences control Conservatism, or that they control Liberalism or "Labour," nor even that they control Communism, but through the effects of Universal Suffrage, they can get control over the whole lot.

They then mould the frame-work of all these political parties to accomplish their objects.

Rabbi I. I. Mattuck understands this clearly. He wrote in the London Chronicle, 14th April 1944:

"The fate of the Jews is bound up with Democracy ... There is an irreconcilable conflict between antisemitism and Democracy ... Antisemitism must be destroyed if Democracy is to prevail ..."

If this means anything, it means that the system of universal suffrage known as Democracy must be made secure for the Jew to maintain his present position. But the Jews, too, give expression to opinions that they believe in the idea of government by an elite, so long as they are the elite. In the Sermon of the Week in the London Jewish Chronicle, 1st January 1943, they show that they know, as well as anybody else, that:

"All great movements spring from the few and early every ideal degenerates with popularity. Every new truth, each new representation of an old truth, as soon as it becomes the property of the many for whom it is intended, loses its inspiring power and becomes a commonplace. For the standards of the many must always be low ones, and it is rarely the best or noblest ideas that can be accepted by the majority."

The idea of Democracy does not receive much support here. But if Democracy can be used to get others to fight your battles for you to maintain your position in a body politic, by all means use it to advantage. To the great detriment of the countries in which he lives, this, the Jew has managed to do.

It is worthwhile here to quote some thoughts on Democracy by famous men:

Lord Macauley's letter, dated May 23, 1857, to the Hon. H. S. Randall, New York City, expresses his ideas about the future of the United States under the democratic system:

"I am certain that I never in Parliament, in conversation, even on the hustings - a place where it is the fashion to court the populace ... uttered a word indicating the opinion that the supreme authority in the state ought to be instructed to (by) the majority of citizens told by the head; in other words, by the poorest and most ignorant of society. I have long been convinced that institutions purely democratic must sooner or later, destroy liberty or civilization, or both."

(After a considerable discourse on how a hungry and 'propertyless' people will succeed in plundering the United States by legislative means, * he continues) ...

"There will be, I fear spoliation ... when society has entered on this downward progress, either civilization or liberty perish. Either some Caesar or Napoleon will seize the reins of Government with a strong hand or your Republic will be fearfully plundered and laid waste by barbarians in the twentieth century as the Roman Empire was in the fifth; with this difference:

"that the Huns and Vandals who ravaged the Roman Empire came from without and your Huns and Vandals will have been engendered within your country by your own institutions."

J. S. Mill- "It is not useful, but hurtful, that the constitution of this country should declare ignorance to be entitled to as much political power as knowledge."

Goethe -"There is nothing more odious than a majority. It consists of a few powerful leaders, a certain number of accommodating scoundrels and subvervient weaklings, and a mass of men who trudge after them without

in the least knowing their own minds."
(What an apt description of the present state of the British Governent.-A. L.)
Clemenceau - "Majority Government means gov ernment by inferior minds, and the slow rate of progress is determined by the necessity to convince inferior minds."
Thomas Carlyle-"Historically - speaking, I believe there was no nation that could ever subsist on Democracy."
My readers may reflect that following the adoption of universal suffrage in 1928 it only took eleven years for Britain to be jockeyed into a war which resulted in the United States becoming the greatest naval power* in the world. Democracy was the means of rotting France before the War.
Now let us look at our Allies. Is Russia a Democracy? Is China a Democracy? With a contempt for their audience that is scarcely without parallel, with cold disregard for fact, and with shameless bare-faced effrontery, our "statesmen" and journalists have been speaking and writing of the Allied Nations as "the democracies"for the last three years. They are not uninformed. They know that they are perverting the facts when they call Russia and China "democracies." Why do they lie? This I will show in the proper place.
How is it that Churchill did not himself protest against this distortion of the facts by his followers, in view of his own opinions on the nature of the Soviets?
In his broadcast on 20th January 1940 he had spoken up for Finland (or for his friends' Nickel Mines there?) in these words:
"Many illusions about Soviet Russia have been dispelled in these weeks of fierce fighting in the Arctic Circle. Everyone can see how Communism rots the soul of a nation; how it makes it abject and hungry in peace and proves it base and abominable in War ... If the light of freedom which burns so brightly in the frozen North should finally be quenched, it might well herald a return to the Dark Ages when every vestige of human progress during 2,000 years would be engulfed."
Churchill wrote of Soviet Russia in his book, GREAT CONTEMPORARIES:
"In Russia, We have a vast, dumb people dwelling under the discipline of a conscripted army in war time; a people suffering in years of peace the

rigours and privations of the worst campaigns; a people ruled by terror, fanaticisms and the Secret Police. Here we have a State whose subjects are so happy that they have to be forbidden to quit its bounds under the direst penalties; whose diplomatists and agents sent on foreign missions have often to leave their wives and children at home as hostages to ensure their eventual return. Here we have a system whose social achievements crowd five or six people in a single room; whose wages hardly compare in purchasing power with the British dole; whose life is unsafe, where liberty is unknown; where grace and culture are dying; and where armaments and preparations for war are rife. Here is a land where God is blasphemed, and man, plunged in this world's misery, is denied the hope of mercy on both sides of the grave - his soul, in the striking protesting phrase of Robespierre -'no more than a genial breeze dying away in the mouth of the tomb.' Here we have a power actively and ceaselessly engaged in trying to overturn existing civilizations by stealth and propaganda, and when it dares, by bloody force. Here we have a state, three millions of whose subjects, are languishing in foreign exile, whose intellingentia have been methodically destroyed; a State nearly half a million of whose citizens, reduced to servitude for their political opinions, are rotting and freezing through the Arctic night; toiling to death in the forests, mines and quarries, many for no more than indulging in that freedom of thought which has gradually raised man above the beast. Decent good-hearted British men and women ought not to be so airily detached from realities that they have no word of honest indignation for such wantonly, callously inflicted pain."

Yes! Churchill said all that! Then whence came this alliance with Russia? From Churchill? It would not seem likely at first sight, would it? But consider this:

Churchill's association with the men of international finance such as Mr. Bernard Baruch in the United States, is a matter of public knowledge through various press 'reportings', Mr. Churchill's father was a Rothschild intimate, as is Churchill himself. The Rothschilds opposed Bolsevism, despite its Jewish inspiration, because through it they lost their Baku Oil field. This led to an opposition of interests between them and other Jewish interests, especially in the United States, who favored Bolshevism. The appearance of Hitler's National Socialist Government on the scene brought about a union of interests for self-preservation. In view of the known facts, does this not appear to explain Churchill's change of view?

The world democratic press did not take much notice that the dismissal of Prime Minister Goga in Romania by King Carol was an act of dictatorship. It rather applauded the dismissal of the King's Minister elected by popular vote who sought to curb the Jewish influence in the affairs of his country. Perhaps Madame Lepescu, the King's Jewish friend, had some influence here.

Not many years ago Britain made a loan of sixteen million pounds to the late Dictator of Turkey, Kamel Ataturk.

Salazar, Dictator of Portugal, and one of the wisest statesmen in the world today, was Britain's very good friend.

Daladier had secured the right to make decree laws in France.

President Roosevelt had sought similar powers in the United States.

None of these people were disturbing to Britain or its people.

But Hitler's National Socialist Government which brought greatly improved social welfare to the people of Germany, according to Douglas Reed (see his DISGRACE ABOUNDING), well that is something different. His Government sought to limit the Jewish influence in the affairs of his country (see Arthur Bryant's UNFINISHED VICTORY).

Well, we Britons simply can't stand that, can we?

Which all goes to show that "We are fighting for Democracy" is but a smokescreen to conceal the real reason for war.

"A few powerful leaders" with "a number of accommodating scoundrels" The leaders of Britain know perfectly well that it is not Democracy that we are fighting for, but for the Power which battens upon it.

* See MARXISM AND JUDAISM, by Salluste.
See THE REVOLUTION WAS, by Garet Garrett.

Chapter X

THE THEORY THAT HIGH FINANCE CAUSED THE WAR

There is a school of though which believes that International Finance with its preponderant Jewish interest and the Monetary System under which most of the world has suffered from mass unemployment was doomed to be superseded by Hitler's credit system based upon a goods standard and international barter. This would displace gold, the tool of the Internationalists.

I believe this myself.

But some go so far as to say that the war was brought about so that, if Hitler could be defeated, the Gold Standard ard Monetary System, which is fraudulent, could be maintained to the benefit of Wall Street and other large Gold Controllers.

I do not believe that.

It might be worth a war from the point of view of Wall Street, but it would not be worth this war. This war shows every trace of our having been dragged into blindfolded and unprepared. Wall Street would not have allowed that. Wall Street knows that if the Germans won the war, there would be no more Wall Street.

In my opinion there was more to it than the survival of the fraudulent Gold Standard System. The necessities of racial survival made it urgent for the Jews to act without delay. Their considerable influence in Wall Street together with other participants in the spoils of the fraudulent system made it not too difficult to get the "Street" to support a war which was represented as inevitable.

This is not the place to go into the intricacies of monetary systems. The kernel of the problem is that credit based upon gold is insufficient for the needs of modern commerce. A short supply of money and credit is best for the usurer or money-lender, since scarcity raises the rate of interest borrowers must pay. Power to regulate the amount of money and credit available enables the controllers of Gold to dominate world affairs, economically and politically. The creation of inextinguishable national debts is part of the system of control and with control goes domination.

This system of economic and financial bondage was doomed by the expansion of the barter system developed by National Socialist Germany.

(For a more detailed explanation see the chapter, The Peace We Lost in A PEOPLE'S RUNNYMEDE, by Robert Scrutton, Andrew Dakers, publisher.)

Chapter Xl

THE OBJECT IS TO DESTROY FASCISM AND HITLERISM

At last we approach facts.

Certainly we went to war with the object of destroying Fascism and Hitlerism. But the people were not allowed to know this till it was too late to withdraw, or they would not have sanctioned it, had they had an opportunity to do so. It was not Hitler or a Fascist form of Government that was objected to but that both opposed the Jewish influence in their domestic affairs.

President Roosevelt, in a letter to the International Labour Office Conference in 1944, said:

"The welfare of the world's population and their liberty are the first and ultimate concern of those dedicated to root out from this earth every trace of Nazi ideas and Nazi methods."

The London Times' leading article of 26th September 1939, said:

"We have gone to war with the single-minded determination to rid Europe of a particular menace whose presence is incompatable with the continuance of civilized life, and it is the simplicity of this claim that resolves what the Duce feels to be inconsistency in our discrimination between Hitler and his Russian accomplice. We believe that the Russian action. lawless and treacherous as we must declare it to be, is a secondary and subordinate consequence of the original crime. The Soviet has not been a party to Hitler's previous outrages and has not shown itself to be in essence an aggressive power."

The Duce was not the only man to see inconsistency in the discrimination in favour of the Soviets, despite this dead-lame explanation.

On plenty of other occasions, politicians have assured us that we are fighting to destroy Fascism. But they do not tell us why they deem it so necessary. There was a time when it did not appear to be a necessity to Winston Churchill. In his Great Contemporaries he wrote:

"Those who have met Herr Hitler face to face in public business or on social terms have found a highly competent, cool, well-informed functionary with an agreeable manner, a disarming smile."

Again in STEP BY STEP, Churchill wrote of Herr Hitler:

"If our country were defeated, I hope we should find a champion as indomitable to restore our courage and lead us back to our place among the nations."

But of Russia, Churchill said in 1920:

"The Soviet system is barbarism worse than the Stone Age."

In a broadcast on 20th January 1940 he said:

"Everyone can see how Communism rots the soul of a nation ..."

And later in the year on 1st April, he said:

"Communism is a deadly mental and moral disease."

From this it is not understandable why Churchill should be leading the British Empire in a war to destroy National Socialism with the aid of Bolshevik Russia.

Of Italian Fascism, Churchill said in a speech on 11th November 1938:

"Italy has shown that there is a way of fighting the subversive forces and rallying the masses of the people, properly led, to value and wish to defend the honour and stability of civilized society. Hereafter no great nation will be unprovided with an ultimate means of protection against the cancerous growth of Bolshevism."

As far back as 1926 the Financial News reported that a Committee of British Residents in Florence announced:

"We wish to state most clearly and emphatically that there exists here today nothing that can be justly termed either tyranny or suppression of personal free dom as guaranteed by constitutional law in any civilized land. We believe that Mussolini enjoys the enthusiastic support and admiration of the Italian people who are contented, orderly and prosperous to a degree hitherto unknown in Italy, and probably without parallel at the present time among other great European nations still suffering from the war."

Sympathetic readers will smile when they are reminded that in 1933 the Financial Times brought out a special eight-page Supplement under the caption:

The Renaissance of Italy

Fascism's Gift of Order and Progress

The solution of the mystery is that in those days Fascism had not yet grappled with Jewish influences dominating the nation's affairs. Guseppe Toeplitz, Polish born Jew, had just retired from the management of the

Banca Commerciale Italiana, which a New York Times dispatch from Milan on January 29, 1938 (the date of Signor Toeplitz's death) estimated controlled one-seventh of all Italian industries.

We Fascists have noticed with amusement how our own Government is forced by the pressure of necessity to adopt many of the policies of Fascism. We may in stance the recognition of Agriculture as basic among the industries; the necessity of ensuring that the Land is not misused by those farming it and the corporative organization of certain industries and professions.

The International Labour Office issued a report in April 1944 in which the activities of the German Labour Front established by Hitler were recommended to be "adapted for future use" after our victory. Facilities for workmen's travel, recreation and other spare time activities, for vocational training and research on labour protection; the "Beauty of Work" service-"Kraft durch Freude" (Strength through Joy) in the National Socialist Labor Program-and the Labour Bank, "one of the chief credit institutions ... of the whole of Europe"; "it should also be the responsibility of the Labour Commissioners," the Report of 1. L. O. further outlines, "to continue all administrative services required for the administration of labor and social legislation-employment services, social insurance and the labour inspectorate." The I. L. O. Philadelphia Labor Charter actually purloins direct from Fascism its notions of industrial organizations! "It insists," says the London Times of 13th May 1944, "on the employers' right to combine freely, and declares also that if workers and employers combine to run industry collectively, there must be a third element - the Government-to co-operate and see that the rest of the community is not exploited." Similar proposals are found in the 1944 Report on Reconstruction issued by the Grand Council of the Trade Union Congress.

It was on these principles that the Fascist Corporative Organization of Industry was based! Then why should we be so keen to destroy all this? There can be but one plausible answer. National Socialism and Fascism opposed the Jewish influence in the domestic affairs of their respective countries. That we have ample proof that National Socialism and Fascism were good governments for the Germans and the Italians of their respective countries, apparently, is of no consideration. Is it that only Jewish interests matter the world over?

We may venture to doubt whether better Government for "liberated" Italy than the Fascists one can be achieved with the material at hand. Just consider this London Times report of the 25th April 1944:

"As most members of the new Cabinet are Republicans, a form of procedure was devised whereby Ministers, before taking oath, signed a declaration stating that they had accepted office with the purpose of serving the best interests of the country, but without attaching any permanent significance to the ceremony."

It was from such "accommodating scoundrels" as this that Fascism saved Italy for twenty years. At the time of this writing, every so-called "liberated" country begins a campaign of violence and outrage against its most active anti-communist elements. The same conditions are at once reproduced from which their Fascist or semi-Fascist Governments of the past had saved them.

Chapter XII

UNPREPARED AND BLINDFOLDED

It is common knowledge that this country went to war without being attacked. If some vital national interest had compelled Britain to start a war against Germany, we should at least have waited until the most favorable moment before declaring it. The fact that we were hurried into war unprepared and blindfolded is circumstantial evidence that we did not go into it to protect some vital interest. Nations which are not under attack do not start wars unless they are pretty well convinced that they can win them.

When Churchill became Prime Minister, he said he could promise us only "blood and tears." As he had so long been one of the most active politicians in favor of "stopping Hitler," the sense of responsibility he owed to the nation should have prevented him from hurrying matters on before he had first made reasonably sure that we had at least the best chance of victory. We can only conclude that someone forced him on from behind-someone to whom this country's welfare was a matter of no great moment.

The Foreign Secretary admitted that we had got ourselves into a mess without any clear notion of how to get out of it, when he said on the 2nd November 1939:

"Unless we know the duration of the war and its intensity, we can form no estimate of what will be the state of Europe when victory is won."

Mr. Oliver Lyttleton, Minister of Production, said at Farnborough on 6th May 1944:

"It was surely a chastening thought that we were now alive as a British Commonwealth and Empire more by the mistakes which the enemy made in 1940 than by any foresight or preparation which We had made before that date."

On the same day Lt. General A. E. Nye, Vice Chief of the Imperial General Staff, revealed at Coventry that

"... those of us who had access to all the information available, who knew the full extent of our unpreparedness, were fully aware that it would take at least two years from the outbreak of war before we could organize, train and equip an army proportion ate to our needs, and we all knew that during those two years we were bound to be involved in a series of disasters."

Then we may ask, why was not the Imperial General Staff consulted before we committed ourselves to come in when Poland called upon us? These three admissions by responsible men prove that those who had been working so hard to bring us to war to "stop Hitler," could not, when they were doing so, see a year ahead. They were blindfolded, or they would not (if they were patriots) have acted as they did. Their objects therefore could not have been connected in any way with the welfare of the country.

Speaking in the House of Commons in 1941, the late Col. Wedgewood, M. P., had to admit:

" ... If Russia surrendered, he doubted whether our resolution would hold for long, so tempting would be Hitler's offers of peace."

Mr. Eden queried:

"Where would this nation be if Russia were unable to hold the enemy?"

The answer to that query would be,

Exactly where he and his fellow-warmongers had put it.

It is not that they did not know that they had no chance without Russia. THEY DID KNOW. The dates and quotations of the following statements prove it:

25th May 1939, Mr. Eden:

"If an effective resistance to aggression is to be organized in Eastern Europe, Russia's whole-hearted co-operation is indispensable." (Birmingham Post.)

22nd June 1939, Mr. Churchill:

"Without an alliance with Russia, no effective stability can be created or long maintained in Eastern Europe." (Manchester Guardian.)

3rd April 1939, Mr. Lloyd George:

"If we are going to help Poland without the help of Russia, we are walking into a trap." (Extract from speech in House of Commons.)

They knew we depended upon the Soviets for possible success, and they knew it months before war was declared by Britain. Not merely did these politicians drag us into it without the foggiest idea of how to "hang the washing on the Siegfried Line," but they cannot offer us any hope even after the war is won. Sir Kingsley Wood warned us, 2nd February 1943:

"A war of such unprecedented devastating and crippling a character must mean that not only this country but the whole world would be much poorer and disabled . . . We should live in a fools' paradise if wishful thinking led us to believe that this cruel war would bring us in its train happier times and better days."

Mr. Duff Cooper, 16th March 1943, said:

"We should do all we could to take away from the programmes that are occasionally put before the world those tremendous hopes of immediate improvement. It is not likely that on the morrow of this war, things are going to be better than they were before. You cannot devote everything to the work of destruction and expect to find as a result a much better, finer world built up."

A "phoney war"?

In we went, unprepared and without hope of improving our position according to the politicians I have just quoted. The people themselves were so puzzled as to why it had to be that the politicians were obliged to keep telling them what the purpose of the war was. And all reasons given were different. We discuss ten of the reasons in the first ten chapters.

But Hitler gave the true reason for the war in every speech he made- International World Jewry.

The Ministry of Information was as uncertain as to what we were committed as any other Department of the Government. In December 1939 it published a pamphlet called "Assurance of Victory," in which it actually said:

"We do not have to defeat the Nazis on land, but only to prevent them from defeating us. If we can succeed in doing that, we can rely on our strength in other directions to bring them to their knees."

How absurd in the light of subsequent events!

That Churchill was just as vague over the silly experiment and its consequences, we saw when, without any Mandate from "Democracy," he offered defeated France an Act of Union in which "France and Great Britain shall no longer be two nations but one Franco-British Union"!

This irresponsible lunacy was turned down by France, and is never now referred to in polite circles. It shows only two plainly that British interests were secondary to something else.

Then there was Japan. Britain was pledged by Churchill to come in "within the hour" if America and Japan went to war. In other words, just as we allowed Poland to decide when we were to go to war with Germany, so we allowed the United States to involve Us in war with Japan. The run of disasters which followed the outbreak, in which we lost Hong-Kong, Singapore, the Malay States and Burma, shows that no proper preparations had been made for this tough proposition either. If we had goine into this war against Japan for British interests, we would have managed it differently*

International World Jewry which thrust us forward into the War was desperate and quite unconcerned with the future of the British Nation.

That the war was forced upon Japan and how is shown in:

THE TRUTH ABOUT PEARL HARBOR and THE FINAL SECRET OF PEARL HARBOR, by John T. Flynn (Strickland Press, Glasgow).

Chapter XIII

HITLER ALWAYS KNEW HIS REAL ENEMY

Throughout the war, Hitler consistently reminded the world who his real enemies were:
October, 1941: "Unfortunately, the nation whose friendship I wanted most did not join in. Their responsibility for that was not with the entire British nation.
There were a few who, in their stubborn hate and craziness had sabotaged every such attempt supported by the world enemy-International Jewry ... The plot of the Democrats, Jews and Freemasons achieved the plunging of Europe into war."
November 1941: "England, inspired by International Jewry and the Soviet Union, also led by Jews."
1st January, 1942: "The driving force behind them (the Allies) is the Jewish plutocrats, who, for thousands of years have always been the same eternal enemy of human order and consequently of a real social justice ... The Jewish Anglo-Saxon financial conspiracy does not fight for any kind of democracy."
30th January 1942: "Mr. Churchill supported by a small clique, has said that I want war. Behind him and his clique stand the Jews who pay them."
24th February 1942: "This close alliance of Jewish capitalism and Communism is not new to us old National Socialists ... By this war, not Aryan mankind, but the Jew will be exterminated. Only after the extermination of the parasites will the world know a long period of collaboration between nations and therefore a period of peace."
26th April 1942: "The hidden powers which incited Britain in the first World War were Jews . . . Bolshevism is called the dictatorship of the proletariat and is, in fact, the dictatorship of the Jews."
30th September 1942: "If Jewry started this war in order to overcome the Aryan people, then it would not be the Aryans, but the Jews, who would be exterminated."*
January 1943: "The alliance between the arch-capitalistic State of the west with the mendacious socialistic regime of Bolshevism is only thinkable

because the leadership in both cases is in the hands of International Jewry. Roosevelt's largely Jewish Brain Trust, the Jewish press of America, the Jewish wireless and the Jewish party organization are nothing more than the equally Jewish leadership of the Soviet Union."

January 1944: "The present struggle will open the eyes of all nations to the Jewish problem. The nations will come to regard Germany's anti-Jewish measures as a precedent well worth following, and as the natural course to take."

Hitler has always understood the Jew and at the Nuremburg Congress in 1937 he made a useful summary of Jewish methods of penetration and control:

"The Jews worm their way into every nation and as business people, their first task is to establish and consolidate their influence in the economic sphere.

After centuries of this process, the economic power thus gained leads to the adoption of severe counter measures against the invaders by their hosts. This natural form of self-defense quickens the Jewish attempt to remove, by means of a camouflaged and slow process of assimilation, not only the main grounds for an attack on an alien race but also quickens their efforts to gain a direct political influence on the country in which they happen to live. Both of these dangerous evils are ignored, partly through economic considerations, and partly through an inherent bourgeois indifference. Furthermore, the warning voices of influential or intellectual circles are just as deliberately ignored. History teaches us that this is always the case whenever prophetic results have an unpleasant character. Thus, with the aid of the language which they have adopted, these Jews are successful in gaining an ever increasing influence on political development. Democracy then establishes the pre-condition for the organization of those terroristic elements known to us as Social Democracy, the Communist Party or the Bolshevist International. Whilst Democracy gradually stifles the vital forces of resistance, the advance guards of Jewish world-revolution are being developed in the radical revolutionary movements.

"The ultimate goal is then the final Bolshevik Revolution, that is to say, not the establishment of a proletarian leadership by proletarians, but the subjugation of the proletarians by their new alien masters ...

"In 1936 we proved by means of a whole series of astounding statistics that in Russia today more than 98 per cent of the leading positions are occupied by Jews ...

"Who were the leaders in our Bavarian Workers' Republic? Who were the leaders of the Spartacist Movement? Who were the real leaders and financiers of our Communist Party? Jews, everyone of them. The position was the same in Hungary and the Red parts of Spain."

And, might be added, who are the leaders of the "British" Labour Party today. Well, the New York Times, 31st August, 1946, prints this:

"Lord Rothschild, 35-year-old millionaire scientist, told this correspondent that he had joined the Labour Party because he had read the books of John Strachey, whom the United States twice tried to expel."

Interestingly, Jewish writers and scholars confirm Hitler's thesis of the origin and development of revolutionary movements. Among these Jewish authorities are such names as Bernard Lazare, Karl Marx, Henri Barbusse, Theodor Herzl and Benjamin Disraeli. In Coningsby, published in 1844, some years before the revolution unsettled Europe, Disraeli wrote

"... that mighty revolution which is at this moment preparing in Germany, and which will be, in fact, a second and greater Reformation, and of which so little is as yet known in England, is entirely developing under the auspices of Jews ..." and"... every generation they must become more powerful and more dangerous to the society which is hostile to them." (Pages 231-2, Century Edition, N. Y., 1903.)

It is here that Disraeli has some interesting things to say about the Jewish race:

"No penal laws, no physical tortures, can affect that a superior race should be absorbed by an inferior or be destroyed by it. The mixed persecuting races disappear; the pure persecuted race remains." (Page 231.)

Chapter XIV

HITLER WANTED PEACE WITH BRITAIN

Both in Germany and in Britain there were many people who did all they could to prevent Britain and Germany ever going to war again. Hitler was one of these, but he insisted that in the making of agreements to secure peace, Germany should be placed on an equal footing with other great Powers. When this was denied Germany left the League of Nations.

In his speech of 26th September 1938, he reminded listeners that he had, up to that date, made five different proposals for the limitation of armaments. All had been rejected. In 1935 and again in 1936 he proposed to reduce the horrors of war by prohibiting bombing of any kind outside the range of artillery on the fighting fronts and by the abolition of tanks and artillery of the heavier sorts. Britain stood to gain more from the proposals than any other nation, but they were turned down. *

"The world," said Hitler on 14th October 1938, "which we are not harming in any way, and from which we only ask that it will allow us to go about our business in peace, has been submerging us for months under a flood of untruths and calumnies."

Eight days later, he said:

"Our aim is to make our people happy once more by guaranteeing to them their daily bread. The work involved is great, and the world should leave us to carry it out in peace."

But the world, as Disraeli said in his famous expression in CONINGSBY,

"... is governed by very different personages from what is imagined by those who are not behind the scenes."

·[See Appendix I1, page 112.]

And who were the personages Disraeli referred to?

He tells us through Sidonia - "the Sidonias of Arragon were Nuevos Christianos" and "No sooner was Sidonia established in England than he professed Judaism" who on his arrival in St. Petersburg, "had ... an interview with the Russian Minister of Finance, Count Cancrin; I beheld the son of a Lithuanian Jew." He travelled to Spain and had an audience" with the Spanish Minister, Senor Mendizabel," and beheld one like himself, "the son of a Neuvo Christiano, a Jew of Arragon." In Paris he "beheld the son of a French Jew" (Sou It) . In Prussia "Count Arnim entered the cabinet, and I beheld a Prussian Jew." (Page 232, Century Edition, 1903.)

"There was no adventurer in Europe with whom he (Sidonia) was not familiar. No Minister of State had such communication with secret agents and political spies as Sidonia. He held relations with all the clever outcasts of the world. The catalogue of his acquaintance in the shape of Greeks, Armenians, Moors, secret Jews, Tartars, Gipsies, wandering Poles and Carbonari, would throw a curious light on those subterranean agencies of which the world in general knows so little, but which exercise so great an influence on public events." (Page 202.)

A scanning of the pages of the Press in any Democratic country over the five-year period from 1933 to 1938 will show that Hitler was not to be allowed to revive his country in peace.

In 1938, the British Legion offered its services to supervise the suggested plebescite in Czechoslovakia. Hitler declared he was willing to invite them over for the purpose. Could a responsible German Chancellor have gone further than that?

We have already commented that the Germans in 1940 had offered to retire their Fuhrer if by so doing they could make peace with Britain (page 20). This offer remained concealed from the British people until Mr. Joseph Davies revealed it in 1943.

On 10th May 1941, Rudolf Hess, Hitler's right-hand man, risked his life in landing from an aeroplane in Scotland in an attempt to inverview a certain nobleman whom he conceived might help him to get the war stopped. "The Fuhrer," he said, "does not want to defeat England and wants to stop fighting." He expressed his horror at the idea of prolonging the struggle and gave his word of honor that Hitler never entertained any designs against the British Empire and did not aspire to world domination. But any negotiations between Germany and England, he said, would have to be conducted on this side by a Government other than Churchill's.

Instead of investigating the possibility of ending the carnage by such negotiations, and sending Hess back with a reply, our Government, with Old Testament disregard of chivalry, treated him as an ordinary prisoner of war and later as a criminal.

In 1939, Lothrop Stoddard, the American authority on Race, made a tour through Germany and Central Europe. He reported that "most Germans think the war is stupidly unnecessary and that the British were sticking their noses into what is none of their business."

"Just think of it," they exclaim, "here we are so busy making over our country and now we have to lay aside most of our fine construction plans to go and fight it out with these damned Englishmen!" (Daily Mail, 9th January 1940.)

"We Germans," Goebbels told him, "don't like this war. We think it needless and silly." (Daily Mail, 13th January 1940.)

In November 1941, Hitler announced:

"After the victories against Poland and in the West, I again decided - and for the last time - to hold out my hand to England and to point out that a continuation of the war could only be senseless for England, and there was nothing to prevent the conclusion of a reasonable peace. Indeed there were no differences between England and Germany except those artificially created."

War, however, had been decreed by international Jewish influences and nothing could stop it. These influences were able to fasten upon the politicians the the catch-cry that no one could possibly trust Hitler or have any dealings with him. He was to be regarded as a pariah.

However, Stalin was wonderful.

That Bolshevism is largely a Jewish creation cannot be denied.

But Hitler was pledged to free Europe from the influence of international Jewry. That made a difference.

We, who knew this, were stowed away in prison so that we could not continue to reveal what we knew.

Chapter XV

HOW BRITAIN WAS EGGED ON TO MAKE WAR

The technique was simple: It was to brand Hitler constantly as an aggressor and then try to make out that it was necessary to "stop" him.
Hitler came to power in 1933.
By that time the policies of Great Britain, France, Russia, the United States and many of the lesser Powers were influenced by personages similar to those Disraeli had written of in 1844 and as pre-Hitler Germany had been. As early as April 1933 I prophesied in The Fascist that the Jewish Money Power "will do all it can to bring Hitler down, and failing all else, will try to drag the Western Governments into a war with Germany by means of its power and penetration of these Governments." This is what ensued, although I never thought the attempt would succeed.

In Chapter XIV I quoted Hitler's conciliatory peace efforts. I will now quote some highly provocative speeches, writings and actions of our "responsible statesmen" from 1933 up to the declaration of war they so ardently desired.

Sir Austen Chamberlain, as his father before him, a spokesman for international interests with Jewish connections, described Hitler's new regime as "Prussian Imperialism with an added savagery - that no subject not of pure Nordic birth was to have equality of rights and citizenship in the Nation to which they belong." (14th April 1933.) This was in the House of Commons and the statement was as irresponsible as it was inaccurate.

Soon afterwards, a Captain Sears removed a wreath which had been placed on the Cenotaph by an emissary of Hitler and threw it in the Thames.

During this year (1933) many anti-German boycotting movements were started by Jews. These were mostly of a commercial nature but even when a German team of athletes came over to the White City in August, an attempt was made to boycott them. It is interesting to note that when the Author of this book advocated a boycott of Jews in 1936, he was proceeded against on charges of seditious libel and public mischief. (But he, of course, is Nordic and native.)

David A. Brown, National Chairman, United Jewish Campaign in the

United States, is reported to have told Robert E. Edmondson, an anti-Jewish pamphleteer, "We Jews are going to bring a war on Germany." That was 1934. Samuel Untermeyer's Anti-Nazi League was then organized into a World Economic Trade Boycott of Germany.

On the 14th January 1934, the Sunday Referee, Jewish owned, referring to a visit of Herr Naberberg from Germany with the object of establishing relations between the Youth Movements of both countries, printed headlines "Send those Nazis back to Berlin" and "Unwelcome Visitors to London."

The Sunday Express demanded that the world should cut off all relations with Germany, trade, social and diplomatic. General Smuts from Cape Town, joined the clamour and on April 18th said "The world cannot allow the Jew to be down-trodden."

With disregard for the sentiments of a friendly country the British Government sent the Jewish Treasury Official S. D. Waley to take part in the Anglo-German financial negotiations in Berlin, November 1934.

In the Jewish Chronicle (London) 22nd February 1935 an obituary notice of J. E. Marcovitch, Jewish Managing Director of the most important newspapers in Egypt, stated that he had "converted the whole Egyptian Press into a real battlefield against Hitlerism."

After four years in Berlin as Ambassador for the United States, Mr. William Dodd refused to attend the Nuremberg celebrations and returned to the States.

When Hitler took over Austria, it was the Jewish publisher Victor Gollancz who "led" the protest in Trafalgar Square.

It was noted about this time that the people who were foremost in re-arming us were the very people who previously had disarmed us. The "No More War" policy was abandoned as soon as it was realized that the Jewish world influence would be seriously curtailed if not actually ended if Hitler could not be defeated.

The Evening Standard in July 1938 published a cartoon holding up the German Aryan Religion to ridicule.

Paul Dreyfus, a French Jew from Mulhausen, where the western branch of the Komintern had been established, stated:

"Before the end of the year, an economic bloc of England, Russia, France and the United States will be formed to bring the German and Italian economic systems to their knees." (La Vie de Tangier, 15th May 1938, Tangier.)

Mr. Neville Chamberlain was not guilty of joining in the clamour to "stop Hitler." But said the Evening Standard, 5th August 1939:

" ... he is being hampered by incessant intrigues. Mr. Eden is now allied to the Fabian-Zionist faction headed by Mr. Israel Moses Sieff with its policy of parlour Bolshevism."

Mr. Phillip Sassoon, of the wealthy and powerful Jewish Sassoon family, and First Commissioner of Works,

"... has been allowing Eden and his satellites to hold meetings in his room at the House of Commons. Eden and Sassoon have been friends for years." (News Review 21st July 1939.)

The principal anti-Nazi political leaders in Britain were Churchill, Eden and Duff Cooper.

Press lies, alleging all sorts of misconduct by Nazis were particularly rife in 1938. One, which, like the rest was found to be quite without foundation, was to the effect that a titled British lady had been stripped and searched on entering Germany at Aachen.

"Red Tape," a civil service magazine, printed an article recommending the deportation of Nazi Germans from England because of their anti-semitism.

The Daily Express of 25th February 1939 declared "Antisemitism is a curse of such a desperate character that we must direct all our energies to destroying it."

By the middle of 1939 we had a Jewish War Minister, Hore-Belisha; the Jewish Nathan was leading the recruiting campaign for the Territorial Forces; the Jewish Lady Reading leading the Women's Services; and the Jewish Humbert Wolfe compiled the National Service Handbook.

No wonder that on April Ist, 1939, Herr Hitler's Wilhelmshaven speech warned the world:

"Only when the Jewish influence that splits the Nations apart has been eliminated will it be possible to bring about international co-operation based on a lasting understanding."

The warning was, of course, ignored. Even the Right bulletin, journal of the Right Book Club, called Hitler "a megalomaniac who, every day he is permitted to continue unchallenged and unchecked, constitutes a grave menace to the security of this realm and our Empire."

A propaganda film, The Confessions of a Nazi Spy, was shown in London. It was an insult to Germany. The director of the film was the Jewish A. Litvak, the technical adviser was Rabbi H. Lissauer, the "historical director" was the Jewish Leon Turrou; and the chief characters were played by three Jewish actors, E. G. Robinson, whose real name is Goldenberg, Paul Lukas and F. Lederer.

At the Socialist Conference at Southport held in May 1939, Mr. Noel Baker confessed that the Socialist Party "wrote messages for the secret German Press which circulates in "Hitler's country."

In the United States before the House of Representatives Committee on Un-American Activities, General van Horn Moseley, sensitive to the Jewish influence in his country gave evidence in the form of a carefully compiled report of Jewish revolutionary activity in the States. The General gave at the same time evidence of a Jewish attempt "to find his price" to remain silent. The Committee ordered that all of the evidence should be excluded from the records of its proceedings! This was done not only as a part of the usual conspiracy of silence on the Jewish influence but also to prevent a sympathetic understanding of the cleansing going on in National Socialist Germany.

Having succeeded in plunging France and the British Empire into war with their enemies, World Jewry, stood aghast when Germany defeated France and threw the British Forces into the sea. The next thing to do was to get the United States into the war or their cause would be lost. Having aided in getting the United States into the last war (see page 77) in a deal with Britain to grant them Palestine as a future National Home, the task was probably not considered without chance of success, as the future showed.

Hollywood took a leading part in this campaign. And Hollywood counts. The whole world watches Hollywood and listens to Hollywood. And the Hollywood film-producing companies are largely Jewish. That is no secret.

Of Hollywood, Senator B. C. Clark asserted on the 10th day of September 1941, that half a dozen men con trolling the film industry were bent on inflaming the American people to clamour for war.

The Daily Express reported, 11th September, 1941:

"Appearing before a Senate Committee investigating propaganda in films, he (Senator Clark) said the industry was turning out dozens of pictures to infectthe minds of their audiences with hatred to arouse their emotions. America's 17,000 cinemas virtually constitute daily and nightly mass meetings for war."

Chapter XVI

THE JEWS ACKNOWLEDGE THEIR POWER AND THREATEN

The line of demarcation between threatening war and waging it is rather indistinct when one of the belligerents is a community sheltering behind the defenses of many different Powers and recognized by these Powers to be their nationals although actually alien to them all. I have, however, endeavored to distinguish between these two conditions, giving proofs of threats in this chapter and proofs of actual waging of war in the next.

The following examples disclose that the Jews believe that they have the power, and will, if need be, to cause international strife:

"If those discussions would result in the destruction of Jewish rights in that country (Palestine) ... a deep despair would settle on the masses of the Jewish people. That would not be a development which sane statesmen could contemplate with unruffled composure. In every deed, they would be confronted by the Jewish problem in a form more acute than at any time in history, and, try how they would they could not escape it. It would thrust up its hydra head at countless places in the diplomatic scene and block every avenue of international appeasement. (Watchman, London Jewish Chronicle, 3rd March 1939.)

Rabbi A. H. Silver described in the London Jewish Chronicle as "one of the greatest leaders of the American Community," speaking at his first meeting in England on a tour for the Second Palestine War Appeal, at Conway Hall on 12th March 1942, made this declaration:

"There would never be peace in Europe until the problem of the Jewish People in Europe was solved.

And the world ought to know that."

This statement was received with loud cheers by the Jewish audience. Under the circumstances in which this statement was made it is an utterance of extreme importance.

At a Zionist Conference, reported 22nd January 1943 (London Jewish Chronicle) the Jewish Berl Locker said:

"They had the right to come to the world today and say 'Here is the Jewish problem which you must solve. Otherwise there won't be any rest in the world.' "

Vladimir Jabotinski, Jewish Zionist leader, at the 5th Congress of Polish Zionist Revisionists at Warsaw said that the Jews might

"... become the dynamite which would blow up the British Empire." (London Times, 30th December 1931.)

A Jew Eberlin wrote in his book A la VEILLE de la RENAISSANCE :

"The Jewish people will not obtain full possession of Palestine until the fall of English Imperialism . . .

Our principal aim, for the moment, is the destruction of British Imperialism."

Dr. B. Messinsohn, lecturing to Zionists at Cape Town, 2nd July, 1930, said:

"I warn the world that if it does not keep faith, there are 16 million Jews who will be filled again with the hatred and despair which released so many destructive forces among them in the days of their great oppression. I warn the world! We are a great Power."

(Cape Times, 3rd July 1930.)

Col. Nathan, M. P., Chairman of the National Defense Public Interest Committee, formed to boost British recruiting, told an audience:

"If Zion falls, the British Empire falls with it." (Jewish Chronicle, 27th January 1939.)

And now for a few statements acknowledging Jewish power in the less recent past.

"We are at the bottom, not merely of the latest Great War, but of nearly all your wars; not only of the Russian, but of every other major Revolution in your history ... We did it solely with the irresistible might of our spirit, with ideas and propaganda." (By the Jewish writer Marcus EH Ravage, Century Magazine, January 1928.)

"There is scarcely an event in modern Europe that cannot be traced back to the Jews. We Jews are to day nothing else but the World's seducers, its destroyers, its incendiaries, its executioners." (By the Jewish scholar, Oscar Levy, in his preface to G. Lane-Fox Pitt-Rivers, The World Significance of the Russian Revolution.)

Goldwin Smith, D. C. L., Professor of Modern History at Oxford, wrote in the Nineteenth Century, October 1881, as follows:

"When I was last in England, we were on the brink of a war with Russia which would have involved the whole Empire ... The Jewish interests throughout Europe, with the Jewish Press of Vienna as its chief organ, was doing its utmost to push us in." (This was the time of the Russo-Turkish War, 1877.)

"The Jew alone," he said further, "regards his race as superior to humanity, and looks forward not to its ultimate union with other races, but to its triumph over them all and to its final ascendency under the leadership of a tribal Messiah."

Col. C. Repington recounts a conversation he had (5th April 1921) with Count Mensdorff, Austrian Ambassador in London in 1914, as follows:

"Mensdorff thought that Israel had won the War; they had made it, thrived on it, profited by it. It was their supreme revenge on Christianity." (After The War, page 155, Constable, 1922.)

"The hitherto unsuspectedly powerful force of Zionist Jewry in America" is revealed by Samuel Landman, member of the Board of Deputies in England and a Councillor of the Zionist Federation, in a letter to the Jewish Chronicle, 7th February 1936 (see another source, page 29). He writes:

"... that the best and perhaps the only way to induce the American President to come into the war was to secure the co-operation of Zionist Jewry by promising them Palestine. By so doing, the Allies would enlist and mobilize the hitherto unsuspectedly powerful force of Zionist Jewry in America and elsewhere in favor of the Allies on a quid pro quo basis."

The promise of Palestine as a National Home for the Jews was made, and

"... The Zionists carried out their part and helped to bring America in. The Balfour Declaration of 2nd November 1917 was but the public confirmation of a verbal agreement of 1916."

Mr. Lloyd George, in the House of Commons. 19th June 1936, confirmed the facts set forth in Mr. Landman's letter with these words:

" ... We decided that it was desirable to secure the sympathy and co-operation of that most remarkable community, the Jews ... In these conditions, we proposed tis (Balfour Declaration) to our Allies. "We have here, on the highest authority, proof that in 1916 the Jewish influence in the United States was the deciding factor in the matter of peace or war for that country.

"Get hold of fifty of the wealthiest Jewish financiers, the men who are interested in making wars for their own profit. Control them, and you will put an end to it all." (Henry Ford, the motor car manufacturer, is reported as saying in the Cleveland News, 20th September 1923.)

Two years before the second world war, The Daily Express of 28th April 1937 (note 1937 date - Ed.), reported that the present Baron Rothschild 3rd was asked by Mr. T. Driberg where he would live when the lease on his Piccadilly home fell in. The answer was:

"Nowhere, probably; I just don't know. Not until after the war, anyway."

Evidently the Baron knew there was going to be a war.

In February 1945 the Jewish Chronicle, in a leading article, made the unguarded statement of "antisemitism, without which this war would probably not have come about."

This is authoritative evidence that we who were persecuted under regulation 18B knew what we were talking about.

Chapter XVII

THE JEWS DECLARE WAR

The Jew has always been at war with the Gentile world. It is not, of course open war. But confirmation can be had in Jewish writings, if you look for it. The success of this secret war depends chiefly on the silence with which it is conducted. There must be no publicity. Their campaign against our world reminds one of the cuckoo which lays its eggs in the nest of the hospitable and unsuspecting hedge-sparrow. The ultimate consequence is the destruction of all the young hedge-sparrows. The Jews have come to power in a similar way. Only the intelligent few recognize them as inevitable enemies. Money is power, and Jewish money soon buys off effective opposition to their presence and their actions.

The general plan is to penetrate every effective means of influencing what is called "public opinion" and then to wear down the morale of his unsuspecting enemy and host by means of unsound ideas. Of these, "Liberty, Equality and Fraternity," "no distinction of race, creed or colour," are the principal shibboleths used to appeal to the inferiority complex of the mob to promote the tolerance of the Jewish influence in our midst. On the Liberal and Socialistic foundations thus secured, they build up *Marxism, Bolshevism, perverted forms of Christianity, and anti-Nationalism disguised as Internationalism, all for the destruction of Gentile civilization. Through control, direct and indirect, over the Press, the Cinema, the Wireless (i. e., radio - Ed.) and the doctrines of masonry, a censorship is imposed upon anyone who has become aware of what is going on and attempts to sound a warning.

By such methods they destroyed 'Tsardom' and replaced it with Bolshevism to become the new ruling class. To undermine the power of their enemies they taught the idea of Communism to the Gentile and sent the old regime crashing at a time of stress and weakness. But their communism is but an idea. In actual practice it is a super capitalism, State Capitalism, under their control. Perhaps this is an explanation why Jewish bankers support the Soviet regime and have been received in Moscow like Kings.

The ultimate objective appears to be a world dominated by Jewish influence supported by an oriental capacity for hatred towards one's opponents and a desire for revenge which it is difficult for the Aryan people to understand. The fate of Hitler, the raping of German women and the looting and plundering of National Socialist Germany is an example of their ferocity and of those who fall under their influence.

"Not in vain," said the Jewish poet Bialik, brother in-law of the Soviet General Gamarnik, likewise Jewish, "have Jews been drawn towards journalism. In their hands it has become a weapon highly suited to meet their needs in their war of survival. JJ (An address at the Hebrew University, Jerusalem, 11th May 1933)

None other than Benjamin Disraeli gives us this authoritative statement, written in 1852 when the revolutionary upheavals of 1848 had been convulsing Europe, on the perpetual war of the Jews against Christian civilization:

"The influence of the Jews may be traced in the last outbreak of the destructive principle in Europe. An insurrection takes place against tradition and aristocracy, against religion and property ... the natural equality of men and the abrogation of property are proclaimed by the Secret Societies which form Provisional Governments, and men of the Jewish race are found at the head of everyone of them. The people of God co-operate with atheists; the most skillful accumulators of property ally themselves with Communists; the peculiar and chosen race touch the hand of all the scum and low castes of Europe; and all this because they wish to destroy that ungrateful Christendom which owes them even its name, and whose tyranny they can no longer endure."*

Apparently 100 years have brought no change in spirit.

On the 24th March 1938, the Daily Express, whose Chairman is a Mr. Blumenfield, printed a huge caption across its front page:

JUDEA DECLARES WAR ON GERMANY

On 2nd January 1938 The Sunday Chronicle printed an enlarged caption:

500,000,000 POUND FIGHTING FUND FOR THE JEWS over an article which said:

"The Jew is facing one of the biggest crises in his troubled history. In Poland, Rumania, Germany, Austria, his back is to the wall. But now he is going to hit back hard.

"This week the leaders of International Jewry will meet in a village near

Geneva to devise a counter offensive.

"Eight hundred thousand Rumanian Jews are now jeopardized. In Hungary it is feared that open Govrnment measures will shortly succeed the fierce unofficial antisemitism in an attempt to force Hungarian Jews to emigrate. Austrian Jews dread similar action.

"Now a united front composed of all sections of Jewish parties is to be formed. It will show the anti semitic governments of Europe that the Jew insists on fair play.

"'Life of Lord George Bentinck", Colburn & Co., London, 1852, page 496.

"The great International Jewish financiers are to contribute approximately 500,000,000 pounds sterling. This sum will be used to fight the persecuting States. The battle will be fought on the world's stock exchanges. Since the majority of the antisemitic States are burdened with heavy international debts, they will find their very existence threatened."

"A Boycott throughout Europe of their export products by way of the retailer may undermine the present uncertain economic stability of several of the antisemitic countries.

Here is an admission of Jewish power and the will to ruin States hostile to them with utter disregard of the trade requirements of the countries of which they pretend to be nationals. It is obvious that a retail boycott in England against German goods would almost immediately because a curtailment of British exports to Germany with resultant unemployment.

Within a month the Goga Government of Rumania hich sought to restrict Jewish commercial control, fell, owing to an economic and financial crisis.

On 3rd June 1938 the influential American Hebrew printed an article with this foreword: "In a brilliantly written article a non-Jewish newspaperman ventures a daring glimpse into the future." The author was Joseph Trimble. It contained the following:

"The forces of reaction are being mobilized. A combination of England, France and Russia will sooner or later bar the triumphant march of the success-crazed Fuhrer. Either by accident or by design a Jew has come to the position of foremost importance in each of these nations.

"In the hands of non-Aryans lie the very lives of millions. Blum is no longer Premier of France ... but President Lebrun is a mere figurehead and Daladier has shouldered the burden just for a moment. Leon Blum is a prominent Jew who counts ... He may yet be the Moses who will guide the French nation (1946, Blum negotiated the French "loan"- Ed.). And Litvinoff? The great Jew who sits at the right hand of Stalin, the little tin-soldier of Communism. Litvinoff has increased in stature until he far outranks any Comrade of the Internationale with the exception of the sallow-complexioned Keeper of the Kremlin.

"Keen, cultured, capable, Litvinoff fostered and promoted the Franco-Russian Pact. It was he who sold President Roosevelt. He has accomplished the ultimate in the diplomatic ken by keeping Conservative England - managed by silk-topped Etonians - on the most amicable terms with Red Russia.

"And Hore-Belisha! Suave, slick and clever, ambitious and competent, buoyant and authoritative his star is rising. He will follow the path of Disraeli into the residence at 10 Downing Street, where the destinies of all the King's men are decided. The rise of Hore-Belisha has been sensational. He is past master of the sagacious use of the public press, having learned his stuff from Lord Beaverbrook. He has managed to keep his own name prominent. This aggressive young man has transformed the British Army from a shaggy, shabby, down-in-the-mouth and round-at-the-heels outfit to a mechanical fighting-machine, which is at war time strength in a world that threatens to become little more than a dung-hill for dictators.

"So it may come to pass that these three great Sons of Israel, these three representatives of the race that has been forced to play Jean Valjean to Hitler's Jevert; these three Jews will form the combine that will send the frenzied dictator, who has become the greatest Jew hater in modern times, to the Hell to which he has consigned so many of 'their kind of people' ...

"It is almost certain that these three nations, bound by numerous agreements, and in a state of viural though undeclared alliance, will stand shoulder to shoulder toward off the subsequent strides of Hitler toward the East. The order that propels a Nazi goose-stepper across the Czech border will be the spark that will once again send Europe to smash.

"And when the smoke of the battle clears away and he trumpets no longer blare and the bullets have ceased to blast, there may be presented a tableau showing the man who played God, the 'swastikaed Christus', being lowered none to gently into a hole in the ground as the trio of non-Aryans intone a ramified requiem, that sounds suspiciously like a medley of the Marsellaise, God Save the King, and the Internationale, blending in grand finale into a militant, proud and aggressive arrangement of Eili, Eili!" (Jewish cry of triumph. - Ed.)

Rabbi M. Perlzwerg, head of the British Section of the World Jewish Congress, told a Canadian audience:

"The World Jewish Congress has been at war with Germany for seven years." (Toronto Evening Telegram, 26th Feb. 1940.)

This statement confirms Samuel Untermeyer's declaration of a "holy war" over Radio Station W ABC on August 7, 1933.

Another confirmation is from Moishe Shertok, speaking at the British Zionist Conference in Jan. 1943:

"The Yishuv was at war with Hitler long before Great Britain and America." (Jewish Chronicle, 22 Jan. 1943)The Yishuv is the Jewish movement in Palestine.

Lord, Strabolgi, on 4th July 1944, said Chaim Weizmann, just before the outbreak of the war, offered Mr. Chamberlain help from Jewry all over the world, including man-power.

Some details of the economic war, as conducted by boycott, follow:

In April, 1934, Mr. Herbert Morrison, Chairman of the London County Council and Leader of the Labor Party, spoke at a ball to raise funds for the Jewish Representative Council for Boycott of German Goods and Services. He said:

"It is the duty of all British citizens who love freedom and liberty to boycott German goods and services."

This is a lesson in international amity. There was also a Joint Council of Trades and Industries with Lord Melchett and H. L. Nathan, now Lord Nathan, both Jews, at its head, which boycotted Englishmen who wanted to sell German goods.

This is a lesson in domestic amity.

There was a Women's Shoppers' League to assist the boycotting, and a British Boycott Organization headed by the Jewish Captain W. J. Webber (who later went bankrupt without assets), for which Mr. J. C. Lockwood, M. P., and Sir George Jones, M. P., spoke.

Meanwhile the World Jewish Congress tried to organize a world boycott of German goods. Across the Atlantic, Samuel Untermeyer was President of the Non-Sectarian Boycott League of America.

All of these acts of economic war were permitted by the Governments of Britain and the United States.

At a meeting organized by the United Jewish Committee to Aid Soviet Russia, held at Grosvenor House in November, 1942, Mr. Beverly Nichols said he thought that:

"When Hitler had said this was a Jewish war, he was saying something which was largely true, in that if it had not been for the pogroms and the constant persecution of the Jews, the world would not have been aroused to a consciousness of the essential evil that was Nazism."

Rt. Hon. Walter Elliott, M. P., speaking at the Albert Hall in a demonstration against the Nazis' treatment of the Jews, October 1942, said:

" . . considered that the atrocities of the Nazis were, more than any other single factor, the cause of Great Britain going to war. He well remembered how, years before the war, Sir Austin Chamberlain drew at mention to the atrocities against the Jews, and warned the world that with such a system, ordinary relations would be impossible."

Neither of these speakers had a word, of course, of the Jewish atrocities against Germany which caused Hitler to destroy the Jewish power in his country.

In making war on Hitler, the Jews had also to make war against the anti-Jewish workers in the Allied countries. Measures were passed through our feeble and sub servient Parliament which were quite un-British and un-precedented in modern times. Every anti-Jewish patriot was branded in the press as a Quisling, and if he was considered important enough, he was arrested. Then with out charge or trial, he was consigned to prison or internment camp indefinitely.

A subservient Home Secretary was secured in Sir John Anderson, and later Mr. Herbert Morrison. The latter politician, of whose racial origin we know nothing, has a queer record as regards war. In the last War he was a conscientious objector. He is responsible for the following words in the Labour Leader, 3rd September 1914, which are quoted here so that the reader may know the kind of man who was given office in 1940:

"Your King and Country need you!

"Ah! Men of the country, you are remembered. Neither the King nor the Country, nor the picture papers have forgotten you. When the military were used against you in the strike, did you wonder if your King was really in love with you? Did you? Ah, foolish ones, your King and Country need you. Need hundreds of you to go to Hell and to do the work of Hell. The Commandment says 'Thou shalt not kill.' Pah! What does that matter? Commandments, like treaties, were made to be broken. Ask your parson; he will explain. Your King and Country need you. Go forth, little solders, go forth, though you have no grievance against your German brother - Go forth, and kill him. He is only a German dog, will he not kill you if he gets the chance? Of course he will - he is being told the same story."

In this war, however, Mr. Morrison exhorted the nation to "GO TO IT." What explanation, other than the Jew is in peril, can be given?

It is not known if Mr. Morrison is a Jew or not. But why would he speak at the all-Jewish "Sedar" Service, 17th April 1939, at the Hotel Astor, New York? Why was he on the Committee of the Annual Meeting for the Jewish National Fund's 1936 Exhibition and Bazaar?

The somersault of Mr. Morrison is no more strange than the somersaults of the Archbishops and of Mr. Churchill in their outlook upon Bolshevism in Russia. It is no more to be wondered at than the somersaults of the peace enthusiasts who forget all about the desirability of Peace when the destruction of the Jewish influence seemed imminent. They rushed the country headlong into war then.

Those patriotic men and women who expressed their opinion that the country was brought into war by Jewish influences were flung into jail by Sir John Anderson. Regulation 18B which made this possible was pronounced on all sides as un-British-the Ogpu Anglicised. Is that why so few Members of Parliament raised their voices against it? Perhaps they feared to find themselves in Brixton alongside their colleague, Capt. A. H. M. Ramsey. The Jewish Chronicle never failed to publish all the news about 18B, true or false. Any feeble attempt on the part of isolated inarticulate people to protest against the treatment of loyal Britons under 18B was stigmatized as "Solicitude for 18B's."

In the "Sermon of the Week," 8th May 1942, the Jewish Chronicle said:
We have been at war with him (Hitler) from the first day that he gained power.' "

The Chicago Jewish Sentinel, 8th October 1942, said:
"The Second World War is being fought for the defense of the fundamentals

of Judaism."

*"See MARXISM AND JUDAISM", by Salluste.

Chapter XVIII

THE JEWISH WAR

In Britain, the Ministry responsible during the months before the War began was largely under Jewish influence. The Prime Minister, Mr. Chamberlain* was not, however, in my opinion, so strongly under this influence. He genuinely tried to avoid war over Czechoslovakia in 1938. His failing health weakened his resistance to the pressure of the war-mongers. Had he resigned in protest possibly he might have made sufficient stir to prevent war. With the exception of a few Ministers in comparatively domestic posts, the whole Ministry had contact with the influential part of the Jewish Community in Britain.

Why all these men acted as they did I do not pretend to know. Some may have acted in ignorance; some because of their ties with masonry. Some may have ceased to think like Britons. All were steeped in the shibboleths of democracy as politicians must inevitably be. None had an inkling of Race, the true basis for Real Politics. I have shown in other Chapters that there is no explanation of their general disregard for their country's interests if they are to be regarded as intelligent and honest. My only object in going further into their Jewish contacts is to take the reader realize the extent of this alien penetration into British political circles. I wish to point out defects in public life with a view to their reformation and to excite endeavor to correct these defects by lawful means because their continuance is a peril.

The Chancellor of the Exchequer was Sir John Simon (now Lord Simon), not Jewish, but with Jewish connections:

"'Mr. Chamberlain's father offered the Jews a valuable tract of land in East Africa free for their National Home. At that time a British settler could get no free land there. He had in fact, to pay a deposit before he could enter the country. His wife is an ardent Zionist. Lord Simon was a regular guest of the late Sir Phillip Sassoon. Lord Simon recently came in for a legacy from the Jewish Sir Strakosch. In February, 1943, when he became Lord Chancellor, he declared at St. Stephen's Club, S. W., "We shall maintain," in the matter of reprisals on the Nazis. "the good

British principle that only those should be punished who are proved to be guilty." This was said in full knowledge that anti-Jewish patriots were at that moment suffering years of imprisonment for no offense and without trial, under Regulation 18B. Later, in a debate on 18B in the House of Lords (London Times, 26 Jan. 1944) he said that 18B was "preventive, not punitive;" here again, he knew quite well that detention cannot be otherwise than punitive. Actually, the detention at first was not merely punitive but sadistic, whilst throughout the years, detainees were only allowed to see their wives, families or friends for half an hour per week in a supervised prison visit.

The Home Secretary was Sir Samuel Hoare. He said in a Rotary Club meeting in 1938 that he found the Jews an asset to Britain.* Like Lord Simon, he was a regular guest of Sir Phillip Sassoon.

Lord Halifax was Foreign Secretary. His son and heir had married the granddaughter of a Rothschild.

At the War Office was Hore-Belisha. One of his Under-Secretaries was the Jewish Sir F. C. Bovenschen. His catering adviser was the Jewish Sir I. Salmon.

As Lord Chancellor we had Lord Maugham, with Jewish family ties through marriage. His Permanent Secretary was the Jewish Sir Claud (now Baron) Schuster.

Lord Runciman was Lord President of the Council; his son and heir had married a Jewess as his first wife.

At the Board of Trade was Hon. O. Stanley, whose brother-in-law was a Rothschild's son.

"'Sir Samuel must have been reading Beverly Nichols' NEWS OF ENGLAND.

Lord Stanhope was at the Admiralty. Though he looks Jewish, here we know of no Jewish connection.

The Secretary of State for India was the Marquess of Zetland, who has Jewish connections by marriage and is a prominent Freemason. His Assistant Under-Secretary was the Jewish Sir Cecil Kisch; his Honorary Financial Adviser, the Jewish Sir H. Strakosch. The Economic Adviser to the Indian Government was the Jewish T. E. Gregory, whose real name is Guggenheim.

Mr. Malcolm Macdonald was Colonial Secretary. He is associated with Israel Moses Sieff in "P. E. P." (See page 9.)

The Dominions Under-Secretary was the Duke of Devonshire. On the Directorate of the Alliance Assurance Company he had as associates the Jews Rothschild, Bearsted and Rosebery. In 1936 the Duke was associated with the management of the Exhibition in the Aid of the Jewish National Fund.

Sir Kingsly Wood, the Secretary for Air, is a strong supporter of "P. E. P." institutions. He has described the Jews as a race we value in this country and whom we always desire to have with us."

The Ministry of Education was held by Earl de la Warr. He is a "P. E. P." associate. His Parliamentary Secretary was Mr. Kenneth Lindsay, once Secretary of "P. E. P." Mr. Lindsay's private secretary was Miss Thelma Cazalet, a Zionist.

Mr. Ernest Brown was Minister of Labour and National Service. He had the Jew Humbert Wolfe as Parliamentary Secretary.

Mr. E. L. Burgin was Transport Minister. He is a solicitor whose firm advises the bankers Lazard Bros.

Mr. H. H. Ramsbotham (now Baron Soulbury) was First Commissioner of Works. His wife is the Jewess De Stein.

The Permanent Secretary at the Ministry of Pensions was Sir Adair Hore, step-father of the Hore-Belisha. War Minister.

For further research we suggest reading of THE JEWS, by Hilaire Belloc.

The French Government was similarly penetrated, influenced and controlled by Jewish interests.

In December 1938 the New York Daily News ran a several columned article on the Jews holding Federal positions in the United States.

As the war developed, certain changes took place in our Government. The chief one was Mr. Winston Churchill becoming Prime Minister in place of Mr. Chamberlain. Mr. Churchill is half American. His family has had close connections with Jewish interests. Mr. Churchill has said that his father, Lord Randolph, had Lord Rosebery as his greatest friend. It is to be remembered that Lord Rosebery was married to a Rothschild. Lord Randolph was the recipient of a "loan" of 5,000 pounds sterling from Lord Rosebery. Accompanied by a Rothschild mining engineer he toured South Africa investing in gold mines. It is said that his profit was considerable. An ancestor, the Duke of Marlborough, is said to have received a retainer of 6,000 pounds a year from the Jewish goldbroker Solomon Medina in exchange for information about the progress of the war on the Continent. This information enabled Medina to rig markets. August Belmont, a Rothschild representative in New York was a close friend of Churchill's maternal grandfather.

Churchill's brother is with the Jewish stock brokerage firm of Messrs. Vickers Da Costa & Co., who handle the Rothschild account. Churchill's daughter married the Jewish comedian Vic Oliver and divorced him in 1945. His son, Randolph, officiated in 1933 as Chairman of the Young Men's Committee of the British Association of Maccabees, an all-Jewish society. Churchill was injured in the United States some years before the war, by misjudging the reversed traffic directions, while there to visit Mr. Bernard Baruch. Mr. Baruch's influence in America needs no comment. From the Jewish Sir H. Strakosch, Churchill received a 20,000 pound legacy in 1944.

Mr. Churchill has long received favorable mention in the Jewish press of Britain. His fight on the Aliens Bill and against the tightening-up of naturalization regulations in 1903-4 received this comment:

"The House of Commons Lobby correspondent of the Daily Telegraph says 'Obstructionists had matters all their own way with the Aliens Bill in Grand Committee yesterday. Clause I was postponed and only a line and a half of Clause 11 was passed. At this rate it will take 165 days to get the measure through. Mr. Churchill, Mr. Trevelyan and Mr. Runciman were in high glee at the success of their tactics.'" (Jewish World, 24th June 1904.)

"Mr. Winston Churchill's splendid fight in Grand Committee against the first Aliens Bill will linger long in the recollection of those who winessed it." (Jewish Chronicle, 15th Dec. 1905.)

"Dr. Dulberg said that the naturalization question was an essentially Jewish one, and that it was the ambition of the bulk of the Jewish aliens who came to this country to be naturalized. He expressed the hope that Mr. Churchill would carry his promises into effect and transform his words into deeds." (Jewish Chronicle 14th Dec. 1906.)

"Mr. (now Sir) Stuart Samuel reminded his co-religionists that in 1903 Mr. Churchill rendered valuable service to them by opposing the Aliens Bill. Mr. Churchill was one of the first to come forward to oppose that Bill, and no one fought against it with greater spirit or greater ability." (Manchester Guardian, 21st April 1908.)

Mr. Churchill later sought regard for his services:

"Mr. Churchill in addressing a Jewish audience at the rooms of the Achei B'rith Society on Sunday evening appealed for their support on account of the work he had done for Jews in connection with the Aliens Bill.

With regard to the first measure on the subject, men like Sir Charles Dilke, Mr. Herbert Samuel and himself had striven their utmost to wreck the bill." (Manchester Guardian, 9th Jan. 1906.)

Mr. Churchill was Chancellor of the Exchequer in 1925 when Britain returned to the gold standard. He admitted in the House of Commons on 17th Nov. 1944 that " ... he had been a consistent friend of the Jews and a constant architect of their future."

Mr. Eden replaced Lord Halifax as Foreign Minister in 1940. Lord Halifax went to the United States with the part Jewish Sir R. I. Campbell to help him. It is no secret that Mr. Eden is a great friend of Litvinoff, Foreign Minister of the Soviets, and of the late Sir Phillip Sassoon, whose mother was a Rothschild. Eden used to "sup" with Sassoon several times a week. Here are some newspaper extracts of Mr. Eden's Jewish political affiliations:

"Those who disagree with the Government are looking with interest to Mr. Anthony Eden and wondering which way he means to go. I learn that Mr. Eden is being attracted by the Planners, the organization called Political and Economic Planning, which names itself P. E. P. for short. Planner No. 1 is Mr. Israel Sieff.

In his Park Lane flat he gives some of the best dinner parties in London. Unleavened bread is the feature of these functions. Mr. Kenneth Lindsay, Mr. Robert Berays and Commander Locker-Lampson are frequent guests. Mr. Amery is also a friend of the Sieffs!

"Members of a Sieff dinner party are usually taken around midnight to some dance in aid of a Jewish charity at one of the big hotels.

"But before leaving the flat Mr. Sieff provides the party with entertainment. They are invited to strip off their tail coats and play ping-pong or else ride on the artificial electric camel upon which Mr. Sieff takes exercise each morning." (Evening Standard, 5th August 1938.)

"Sir Phillip Sassoon, First Commissioner for Works, is the latest Minister to be involved in controversy with the Premier. Mr. Chamberlain discovered that Sir Phillip had been allowing Anthony Eden and his satellites to hold meetings in his room at the House of Commons. Eden and Sassoon had been friends for years."

(News Review, 21st July 1938.)

The pedigree of the Schaffalitsky in Mr. Eden's name is not known.

Certain transfers to other posts took place among men I have already mentioned. Of new blood were:

1. The Minister of Food, Lord Woolton, ex-manager of the Jewish firm of Lewis's, Ltd.

2. Minister of Information, Sir J. Reith. Sir John is married to one of the Oldhams family of the Daily Herald. The Jewish Elias (Baron Southwood) has an important interest here.

3. Mr. Ernest Bevin as Minister of Labour. He was Deputy Chairman of the Daily Herald under Baron Southwood.

4. Sir J. L. Gilmour, as Minister of Shipping. He is a member of the Jewish stockbroking firm of Joseph Sobag & Co.

5. Lord Hankey, Minister Without Portfolio to the War Cabinet. The Sunday Express, 26th June 1922, and the Jewish Guardian, 30th June 1922, have mentioned him as being Jewish.

6. Mr. Brenden Bracken, Minister of Information after Sir J. Reith. Mr. Bracken was lately Managing Director of the Jewish-controlled Economist. He recently received a legacy from the Jewish Sir H. Strakosch.

7. Mr. Alfred Duff Cooper, after a lecture tour of the United States to condition the American mind for war, became Chancellor of the Duchy of Lancaster. As one of the most ardent advocates of armed opposition to Hitler, his child was favored by having the late Otto Kahn, of the New York banking firm of Kuhn-Loeb, become its god-father.

8. Mr. J. A. de Rothschild became Joint Parliamentary Secretary, Minister of Supply in 1945.

This is by no means a complete account of the Ministerial changes, but it will serve to demonstrate the sortof people who formed our Government during the War.

The success of a politician depends on his working for the maintenance of the Jewish influence and never opposing it. Little wonder that the scope of this influence is with held from the British people. Any politician breaking the Conspiracy of Silence risks his freedom and perhaps his life. Capt. Ramsay has thus far escaped with the loss of his freedom.

In the narrow strata of our national life that I have reviewed I have shown how the complacent Gentile politician finds it well paid to speak of Jews as injured innocents with never a part in the corruption of ideas, national degeneration, or bloody revolution. The controlled press, radio and cinema, is ever at his command. But native Britons daring to oppose being smothered by this alien influence are treated as criminals. It is anti-Gentilism that goes aided, abetted and unchecked everywhere in official circles.

That similar influences abound in the Governments of the United States and Russia is not unknown to us here in Britain, but my purpose will be served by pointing out that nearly all the important agents sent to this country by these Governments have been either Jewish or accompanied by Jewish advisers.

The Soviet Ambassador in London for the first years of the war was the Jewish Maisky ; the present Ambassador is Feodor Gusev (Joseph) , The Allies are scarcely allowed to speak with one another except through their Jewish emissaries or men with Jewish wives. The Soviet Foreign Office has always been staffed with Jews or their complacent tools. Maxim Litvinoff, man of many aliases, ran it for years. The Daily Telegraph reported, 9th April 1937, "Since M. Litinoff ousted Chicherin, no Russian ever held a high post in the Commissariat for Foreign Affairs."

This paper overlooks that Chicerin's mother was a Jewess. Molotov, the Foreign Minister, has a Jewish wife. One of his two assistants is the Jewish Lozovsky. Lozovsky renewed the Kamchatka fisheries treaty with Japan in 1942. This was a considerable aid to the country Churchill arranged with Roosevelt to bring into the war against us.

Litvinoff was the Soviet Ambassador to the United States from 1941 to 1943; the Jewish B. E. Stein to Italy until relations were severed by war; the Jewish Yureneff to Germany and the Jewish Souritz to France. The influence is carried over into the army - the Russian soldier bears on his cap the five-pointed Star of Judah. The press reported the Jewish General Chornyakhovsky as leading the Soviety Army into East Prussia. The reconquered Ukraine has the Foreign Commissar, the Jewish D. Z. Manuilsky, an old associate of the Jewish Bela Kun, leader of the Red Terror in Hungary. As the Soviet armies drove through Hungary, the Jewish Komlosi was Commissar in Szeged and the Jewish Sobesi in Debreczen.

Mrs. Churchill was met by the Jewish Mme. Molotov and the Jewish Maisky on her arrival in Moscow in 1945. Stalin's second wife is Jewish and the Jewish Kaganovitch has been his right hand man.

In the United States, Mr. Cordell Hull is influenced by his Jewish wife. Mr. Sol Bloom is Chairman of an important Foreign Affairs Committee. The Jewish L. Steinhardt was Ambassador to Russia. He has since been shifted to Turkey. Aiding greatly in preventing Poland from coming to an agreement with Germany over the Geman city Danzig and the Corridor was the half Jewish Ambassador to France, W. C. Bullitt.

The Jewish R. E. Schoenfeld has filled the position of American Charge d'Affaires to the various sham Allied "Governments" in London. Mr. Bernard Baruch, the American "elder statesman" has functioned in various advisory capacities in the mobilization of the war effort in that country. The United States Treasury is directed by Henry Morgenthau, Jr., author of the infamous Morgenthau Plan. The Jewish Dr. H. Aboulker concealed in his house British and American agents preparing the Allied invasion of French North Africa. The Jewish political columnist Walter Lippman instructs the American public how to think politically. Britons are weary of the phrase in the Times "as Mr. Walter Lippman says." Mr. Lippmann told the American Society of Newspaper Editors (21st April 1944) that the peace of the world would be kept by the United States, Russia and British Empire in a permanent alliance.

In Italy, the fall of Mussolini was brought about by the Jewish Bottai and the half-Jew Ciano, and the Gentile Grandi. Bodoglio, who was held up as the nation's leader, is said to be Jewish (Opinion Magazine, Rabbi Stephen S. Wise, editor, Nov. 1939).

"General Tito" of Yugoslavia made the Jewish Moishe Pyade his Vice President; the Jewish Dr. A. Berkania his Supreme Judge; his Adviser on Foreign Affairs is a man by the name of Levy and his Financial Adviser the Jewish Mikloshi. Slovene partisans (the "Liberation Front") have the Jewish leaders Bebler, Kidric, and Vidmar.

The French Government of de Gaulle has contained the following known to be Jewish: Rene Meyer, Minister for Communications; Mendes France, Minister for Justice, replacing J. Abadie, known for the judicial murder of M. Peucheu; Pierre Bloch, Under-Secretary of the Interior; Alphand, Director of Economic Affairs; J. Koenig, Commander-in-Chief of the

French Forces from June 1944, and Carsain and Monthoux, secretaries of De Gaulle. The Director of the Press Bureau of the War Ministry at Algiers is the Jewish Georges Meyer; the Mayor of Algiers, 1945, is the Jewish S. Leber, Director of the Bank of Algiers.

In Abyssinia the Jewish Norman Bentwich visited the country to advise the Emperor on the Constitution he was to have. As a result an almost completely Jewish administration was installed for the Emperor. Prof. Kamrat is in charge of Education; the Messrs. Tedesco and Katz manage Finance; N. Marion is Minister of Justice; Dr. A. Schalit is Minister for Health and Ulendorf manages propaganda for native consumption.

In Eritrea a Mr. Greenspan is Public Prosecutor. When Russia proposed terms for an armistice with Finland in 1944 the communication was made through Marcus Wallenberg, a prominent Jewish financier in Sweden (Times, 6th March 1944). It was through Wallenberg that the United States arranged to curtail the supply of Swedish ball-bearings to Germany.

In the Ukraine, as in many other countries, the guerillas were largely Jewish. It was their activities which led to the reprisals we have heard so much about.

The Inter-Allied Committee of Co-ordination, an organization "mainly concerned with propaganda for the United Nations," has as its Secretary the Jewish A. Hamwee, who was arrested in Buenos Aires in June, 1944, on suspicion of engaging in espionage.

"Liberated Belgium" had the Jewish Gutt as Finance Minister. His confiscatory decrees are well known.

To "Liberated Greece" was sent the Jewish Sir S. D. Waley to advise on the new currency. As a result Greece is now enslaved under the Gold Standard.

As the Allies burst through Germany, Jews were placed in important administrative positions. The Jewish Winkler became Police Commissioner in Cologne. The Jewish H. Fried became the American Military Governor of Hanover.

Henry Morgenthau, Jr., is author of the Morgenthau Plan, the basis of the Potsdam Declaration.

The London Economist, 28th August 1945, wrote of the Potsdam Declaration:

"The conviction that the peace proposal at Potsdam is a thoroughly bad peace is not based on any sentimental softening toward Germany. It is based upon the belief that the system proposed is unworkable. It offers no hope of ultimate German reconciliation. It offers little hope of the Allies maintaining its cumbrous controls beyond the first years of peace. Its methods of reparation reinforce autarchy in Russia and consummate the ruin not only of Germany but of Europe. Above all it has in it not a single constructive idea, not a single hopeful perspective for the post-war world."

Senator William Langer (North Dakota) said in the U. S. Senate:

"Mr. Morgenthau now stands convicted before the case the instigator of systematic annihilation of the German-speaking peoples. The record further proves, beyond any question of doubt, that these fanatical and reactionary high priests of hate and vengeance will never be able to defend their conspiracy before the bar of human reason or human decency. (Congressional Record, April 18, 1946.)

Colonel Bernard Bernstein is the chief cartel investigator for the United States Army.

U. S. District Judge Simon H. Rifkind was appointed Special Adviser to General Eisenhower (and later to Gen. Joseph T. McNarney) after the late General Patton had belittled de-nazification by declaring that he had "never seen the necessity of the denazification program."

(New York Times, 23rd Sept. 1945.)

On the 24th September 1945, the New York Times editorialized as follows:

GENERAL PATTON ON POLICY

"General Patton is a fine soldier. He has won the well deserved gratitude of the American people for his brilliant military leadership. But General Patton is now head of the Military Government of Bavaria, and what he says on the subject of occupation policy is certain to affect both the attitude of our own troops and the response of the German people. When, therefore, General Patton belittles the very purpose for which the war in Europe was fought - namely, the denazification of Germany - we do not believe that his remarks should go unchallenged either by his commanding officer, General Eisenhower, or by his superiors in Washington."

This editorial opinion by an authoritative newspaper in the United States, owned by Mr. Arthur Rays Sulzberger, the Jewish publisher, is but a confirmation of our own opinion that the war was Jewish denazification brought with it Jewish administration everywhere.

The Soviets appointed the Jewish Scheinine as criminal investigator in their zone in Berlin.

Wherever the Allies "liberate" there arises at once confusion, want and anarchy. When the occupying power is Russia, no individual opposed to Bolshevism can hope for anything better than starvation. For the less lucky, there is deportation and a nameless death in prisons, internment camps and mines. The Bishop of Gloucester at the Church Assembly in February, 1945, described how the Russians were attempting to destroy the people and their Churches in Latvia and Esthonia. The greater part of Europe is already in the grip of Bolshevism. When the European countries were "liberated" by the British and American Forces, impotent governments of any shade from pink to red were formed. The people starve and, except where the Allied troops compel order, barbaric bestiality, formerly kept under disciplined control by the Fascist and National Socialist governments, is again let loose. The exploits of the "Underground" are extolled in the liberal democratic press while the efforts of the law fully constituted governments to control this menace to their security were subjected to the vilest calumnies. What connection there is between this anachronism and the large number of Jewish names appearing in reports of "Underground" activities is left to the reader's judgment.

Clearly an attempt is to be made to bolshevise Europe. Starvation is the best foundation for a bolshevist revolution. Is this why starvation always follows "liberation"? We have seen how UNRRA and the provision for supplies is largely under Jewish control. It is worthwhile giving thought to the long occupation of the French ports by the German garrisons. As the Russians advanced into Germany from the East they liquidated the garrisons of the Baltic ports as soon as they were able to. I make the suggestion that the passive policy adopted by Britain and America with regard to the French ports may not have been imposed by military considerations at all, but by the Supreme Power behind the Allies, to ensure the non availability of the ports and the starvation of the "liberated" peoples, with the object of facilitating bolshevisation.

This Chapter will not be complete without a few words about two orders from General Eisenhower. The one, insisting on unconditional surrender, and the other, enforcing non-fraternization with the Germans.

Our unconditional surrender policy prolonged the war far beyond what was necessary. It caused thousands of needless casualties. It ensured the annihilation of many ancient and modern cities, with the roads, railways and canals serving them. No Allied interest could possibly benefit. By ruining Germany, we ruined a market for our own goods.

As for the non-fraternization order, one would have thought that if the German mentality had been as distorted as it was claimed, a good cure would have been friendly talk between "enlightened Allied soldiers and the benighted antisemities of Germany. Then the latter might realize how mistaken they were.

But from the Jewish denazification angle, the ruin of Germany, the destruction of her culture and the massacre of her fighting men in battle mean nothing to an Old Testament outlook steeped in the Asiatic mentality of revenge and extermination.

Fraternization would speedily have made the Allied fighting men conscious of the Jewish influence for which they had been driven into battle. Through fraternization they would really have discovered for what they had been fighting! No, it was necessary to maintain the non-fraterization order until most of the keenest of the Nazis had been wiped up, and that was what was done. Non-fraternization is entirely contrary to all ideas of British chivalry and remote from Aryan British spirit.

Chapter XIX

THE PEACE BRITAIN DEFEATED WHOEVER WINS

Had peace come by negotiation or stalemate, Britons would then have been able to deal with the Jewish influence dominating the affairs of their country. Then there would have been a good chance for a brilliant British future.

But the United Nations won outright, thus enabling the Jewish influence at once to achieve complete World Domination through the Governments of the United States, Russia and the British Empire. This influence in Russia will control the continent, and the United States will hold the rest of the world in debt bondage.

"The United States, the greatest naval Power in the world," admits the Times, 31 August 1944. "It is undeniable," says this paper, 11th Nov. 1944, "that the thread running through all American thinking on this subject is that the age of sea-power was Britain's and the age of air-power is to be America's."

Russia has already shown that whenever she desires, she can shoulder Britain out of her way. She made war on Bulgaria without consulting us at the very moment when our emissaries were conferring with Bulgarian representatives on the terms of a peace. Let Churchill's own estimates of Soviet intentions be quoted from his GREAT CONTEMPORARIES (1937, page 168):

"No faith need be, indeed may be, kept with the communists. Every act of goodwill, of tolerance, of conciliation, of mercy, of magnanimity on the part of the governments or statesmen is to be utilized for their ruin. Then when the time is ripe and the moment opportune every form of lethal violence from mob revolt to private assassination must be used without stint or compunction. The citadel will be stormed under the banners of Liberty and Democracy; and once the apparatus of power is in the hands of the Brotherhood, all opposition, all contrary opinions must be extinguished by death. Democracy is but a tool to be used and afterwards broken."

Yes, that was Churchill, the British Bulldog, the Saviour of Humanity! who announces that Britain's policy is to maintain unbroken friendship with the devils he describes! He allows his underlings to delude the masses with the catchword "Bolshevist Bogey." Stalin's intentions have been clearly stated by him in LENINISM (Allen & Unwin, 1942) : they are to build up in Russia a "dictatorship of the proletariat" so mighty that it can confront the "bourgeois" States with invincible power. Then that power will be used against them. The dictatorship is not the proletariat at all-the proletariat is powerless. The real power is the Jewish influence. Already the plans are laid.

Although there is now some public knowledge about the evils of the Gold Standard, thanks to the pioneering efforts of the late Arthur Kitson, sufficient perhaps to prevent the adoption by this country of a direct Gold-Standard, there is some likelihood that a camouflaged Gold Standard may be foisted upon us. Henry Morgenthau, Jr., evolved some such plan at the International Monetary Conference at Bretton Woods in 1944. Discussion of this in the House of Commons was prevented by trickery. Wall Street will go along with Jewish controlled gold-producing interests of South Africa and with the Soviets. The weapons of domination will be:

1. Gold
2. Inextinguishable Debt.

A peace of domination may be enforced by means of an International Airforce maintained by the Jewish influenced United Nations Organization. The Earl of Harewood, Grand Master of the United Grand Lodge of England, at the Annual Investure of Officers of Freemasonry, 26th April 1944, expressed the hope:

"... that before the next Festival, Europe would be secure, and that these officers appointed that day would enter into a year in which the principles of Freemasonry and their influence would be able to play a valuable part in the peace settlements throughout the world."

Thus we have on the authority of the Grand Master that Freemasonry is political and that the Grand Lodge is part of a world-wide organization.* In 1937 King George VI accepted Freemasonic office at the hands of a subject. That is virtual abdication. It is a point to consider if everything the Government has done since has been illegal, including the precipitation of the Empire into a war and the indefinite imprisonment without trial of patriotic men and women who sought to prevent it.

Sir Stafford Cripps, whose leanings towards Marxism are well known, made this interesting statement about the coming war at Ipswich, 13th October 1935:

"If war comes, as come it may, that war has to be used for the destruction of Capitalism. It will have to be used by the workers in this country to undermine the whole system."

A regularly issued Government Postage Revenue Stamp, in addition to showing the crowned head of King George VI, which is customary, carries five important Masonic symbols - the Square and Compass, the Trowel, the Setting Maul, a Sprig of Acacia carried by the Dove of Peace and a looped Cable Tow. This official recognition of Freemasonry does much to indicate in what high regard the Fraternity is held in that country. To win such an honor is abundant proof that the influence of Masonic principles and teaching are reflected in the vision, progress and welfare of the nation. (From the Masonic Chronicler, Waterloo, Wisconsin, U. S. A.). [The public] do not know that ABSENTEE OWNERSHIP and USURY are their real enemies. The English authors, Arthur Penty and Hilaire Belloc are worth reading on this subject.

Important Zionists forecast with confidence that Britain is to be forced to yield Palestine to the Jews after the war. For example, in the New York Times of January 3rd, 1946, Louis Lipsky, of the World Zionist Executive Committee, warned Britain that "an axe may be driven" into the British Imperial line to India. At this rally at Carnegie Hall, sponsored by prominent American Zionists, Hungarian-born Rabbi Stephen Wise, pointing at the banners in the hall bearing the legend "American Chalutzim Ready to Build and Defend Palestine" and "Aliya, under all circumstances," declared:

"We mean exactly what that says," adding, "and no government can prevent it,"

Evidently the Jews can arrogantly threaten the governments of the world and be lauded for it but criticism of them is forbidden. There is to be "free speech" on every subject except their own international intrigue which keeps the world in a turmoil.

Congressman Patterson has introduced a bill, H. R. 6897, June 27, 1946, in the House of Representatives in the United States which is to make any criticism of Jewish activities punishable by fine and imprisonment.

In both England and the United States patriots have been imprisoned for such criticism. It is not yet possible to execute them as in Soviet Russia (where criticism of Jewish activities is a capital offense) and as Peucheu was judicially executed in North Africa. However, it is unlikely that there is enough informed opinion in either country to offer any serious resistance to such a policy.

*See MARXISM AND JUDAISM, by Salluste.

Chapter XX

CONCLUSION

I have shown in the foregoing pages that every ostensible "cause" for this war given by politicians and press is false.

It was a JEWISH WAR OF SURVIVAL.

The nations that were fighting were forced into it by the Jewish Influences of "Democracy" and of Bolshevism The People are quite unable to protect themselves against the influence of Organized World Jewry under the democratic system.

The stupid doctrine that to be anti-Jewish is to be pro-German has been preached by some of our Parliamentary politicians. That such is not true is shown by the words of Rev. C. B. Mortlock, preaching in Westminster Abbey 2nd January 1943 on the occasion of the offering of a special prayer for the "persecuted" Jewish people. He said:

"How often do you come across the man who is willing to do everything possible to defeat the Germans utterly, yet admits he has some sympathy for Hitler's denunciation of the Jews." (Jewish Chronicle, 8th January 1943.)

Hundreds of decent British citizens were jailed for years without trial or charge simply because they were aware of the menace of the Jewish influence and its methods of working. They were dangerous to Jews, not to their country. They were loyal to their own race when the Government was not "The Bolshevist Bogey" is no ghost story, but a Jewish inspired reality. *

Sir George W. Rendel said:

" ... antisemitism in Europe is one of the things the United Nations are fighting to destroy. We hope to establish in Central Europe countries without racial theories."

Similarly, in June 1944, Mr. Michael Foot said at a meeting in Grosvenor House:

"When the armies of the United Nations go back into Europe, one of their main purposes must be to stamp out the antisemitic creed which had been preached by Hitler."*

"One of the things"! "One of the main purposes"! It was the ONE AND ONLY PURPOSE, since none other can be substantiated.

Even the Jewish Chronicle agrees with this conclusion in its leading article of 2nd February 1945, which peaks of "anti-semitism, without which this war would probably not have come about."

Well, it DID come about, and the result is the sheer devastation of the best part of Europe and its domination by Bolshevism, whilst the British Empire, nearly ruined and rotten to the core with Jewish influences, sinks back to the position of a second-class power.

I am glad to have done the little that was possible to try to prevent all this and regret only that the Jewish influence acting through the power of Money and Propaganda in the opposite direction, has won the first round hands down, by sacrificing millions of Gentile dupes in a JEWISH WAR OF SURVIVAL.

The Jews will also win the next round unless those of us who possess intelligence and character will use both and realize as Disraeli wrote-ALL IS RACE, and seek to eliminate from our civilization and culture the Jewish influence which has caused the great bloody schisms between the western peoples of kindred race and spirit.

Mr. Atlee, moving the resolution for ratification of the San Francisco plan for peace, said: "Although the agreement prevented the world organization from interfering in the domestic affairs of any country, he was sure that it would act swiftly if, for example, there was ever such another outrage as the treatment of the Jews in Germany by Hitler."

*See MARXISM AND JUDAISM, by Salluste.

Appendix I

THE WAR OF EXTERMINATION

It is timely to comment on the expression War of Extermination which appears in Hitler's speeches as the bombardment of civilian populations from the air increased in intensity.

In Hitler's peace offer of March 31, 1936, the limitation of aerial warfare beyond the range of medium heavy artillery was sought. The offer was rejected. *

On Friday, May 10, 1940, the open town of Freiburg, outside the zone of military operations, was bombed by the aeroplanes of the Western Powers. Fifty-three civilians including twenty children playing in a public garden were killed and 151 civilians injured. Mr. Taylor of the American Red Cross reported the incident in the New York Times of May 13, 1940.

This was the first bombing of civilian populations in defenseless towns outside the zone of military operations. The Germans protested and continued to protest, without retaliation, as Allied planes continued the bombardment of civilian populations. After some months the German military authorities warned that the retaliation not yet resorted to would come if bombing of civilians and unprotected cities outside the battle zones continued.

The bombing did not cease.

It would appear that it did not cease because the Allies sought retaliation for propaganda purposes. Retaliation came with the bombing of London in September, 1940.

Hitler's desire to limit aerial warfare to battle-zones had been set at naught. *

With the increasing bombing of civilian population Hitler's addresses began to mention the war of extermination. The Allied purposes gave all the appearances of an endeavor to exterminate the German population. (The senseless and almost complete obliteration of Dresden, one of the most beautiful cities of old Europe, February of 1945, is certainly an indication of the intent. Crowded with refugees fleeing the Bolshevik terror in the East, many thousands of civilians were killed. Subsequent events since the termination of the conflict serve only to strengthen belief in a planned program of extermination.) The Germans began to take counter-measures against those within their reach whom they considered responsible.

Had not Samuel Landman written in his pamphlet GREAT BRITAIN, THE JEWS AND PALESTINE (New Zionist Publications, London 1936): "... the fact that it was Jewish help that brought the U. S. A. into the War on the side of the Allies (1917 - Ed.) has rankled ever since in German,especially Nazi minds - and has contributed in no small measure to the prominence which antisemitism occupies in the Nazi program." ?

Of the making of the peace of 1919, Dr. E. J. Dillon of the London Daily Telegraph wrote in his book THE INSIDE STORY OF THE PEACE CONFERENCE (Harpers, 1920) that the delegates to the Conference from Eastern Europe set down the formula:

"'Henceforth the world will be governed by the Anglo-Saxon people, who in turn are swayed by their Jewish elements' ... and who regard it as fatal to the peace of Eastern Europe." (Page 497.)

Had not Samuel Untermeyer made for World Jewry a declaration of war against Germany over the American radio station W ABC on August 7, 1933, when he spoke of "... the holy war in the cause of humanity in which we are embarked"?

Did not the Jewish author, Theodore N. Kaufman, in his book GERMANY MUST PERISH (Argyle Press, Newark, N. J., 1941) recommend the extermination of the German people by sterilization?

Can the Jews blame other than themselves for all that
has happened to them in Europe?

Hitler, in his speeches, spoke of the international aspects of the Jewish people as a man who had to deal in daily affairs with this problem as a world force effecting his country. His addresses are available to anyone who will take the trouble to read them. But there are better theoreticians on this matter than Hitler.

One is the Israelite scholar Bernard Lazare, already mentioned on page   Another is Theodore Herzl and from him I will quote but one short paragraph:

"When we sink we become a revolutionary proletariat, the subordinate officers of all revolutionary parties, and at the same time, when we rise, there rises also our terrible power of the purse." (The Jewish State, page

26, Central Office of the Zionist Organization, London, 1934.)
Hitler never wrote anything more devastating than that.

*See Appendix Il, page 100.

Appendix II

WHAT THE WORLD REJECTED-HITLER'S PEACE OFFER OF APRIL 1, 1936

In 1936 Hitler sent notes to the British government advocating outlawing of the bomber type plane and of air bombing.

In Geneva, Anthony Eden, then British Foreign Secretary, defended the bomber as an "effective and humane police weapon" in maintaining law and order among the unruly tribes in some of the British colonies.

On April 1, 1936, according to records of the Geneva League of Nations, Joachim von Ribbentrop, then German Ambassador to London, delivered a note from Hitler on a European pacification plan in which, among other proposals for limitation of arms, he proposed:

Prohibition of dropping of gas, poisonous or incendiary bombs.

Prohibition of dropping bombs of any kind whatsoever on open localities outside the range of medium artillery on fighting fronts.

Prohibition of bombardment with long-range guns of places more than 12 miles distant from battle zones.

Abolition and prohibition of artillery of heaviest type.

The note added:

"The German government hereby declare themselves prepared to accede to every such arrangement insofar as it is internationally valid.

"The German government believes if only a first step is taken on the road to disarmament, this will have an enormous effect on relations between nations and consequently to the return of that atmosphere of confidence which is the prior condition for the development of trade and prosperity."

Eden, in his reply to von Ribbentrop five weeks later, on May 6, 1936, said the German memorandum "is most important and deserving of careful study." (Excerpt from Karl von Wiegand's cable from Rome, 19th Nov. 1946, to the New York Journal-American.)

Appendix III

NUREMBERG TRIALS

2nd October 1946
The Editor of The Times (London)

Sir:
Judged by the Nuremberg Law many of the men most honoured in history must be adjudged felons deserving of hanging. If aggression and fomenting war between states is criminal, it would seem strange to posterity that Napoleon's remains should rest enshrined as on an altar beneath the dome of the Invalides while Ribbentrop's are buried beneath a gallows. Among the charges brought against this particular accused is that he helped his fellow Germans of the Sudetenland against the Czechoslovak government. But Cavour, Mazzini and Garibaldi devoted their lives, with the general applause of posterity, to fomenting insurrections among the Italians of Lombardy and Venetia against their lawful Austrian sovereign.

Another of Ribbentrop's "crimes" was signing the order incorporating Austria in the Reich. Apart from the fact that this was done with the approval of at least a considerable body of Austrians, wherein is the unfortunate German's guilt greater than that of Dr. Jameson's who in 1896 levied war on the Transvaal; or that of Cecil Rhodes and Sir Alfred Milner, both of whom certainly worked for the destruction of the two Boer Republics and their incorporation in the British Empire? We did not hang Jameson when he was handed over to us by the Boer government.

Americans know too, that many of their countrymen held that Lincoln was not justified in coercing the seceding states by force of arms. Then he, with Sherman and Sheridan, the authors of the practice of "frightfulness" in war, should hang in effigy beside the former German ambassador to the Court of St. James.

Another charge against the ex-diplomat is that he approved the lynching of allied aviators carrying out machine-gun attacks on the civilian population. There are still British people who believe this form of attack was peculiar to the other side. I remain,

Yours faithfully,
EDMUND B. D'AUVERGNE.

Appendix IV

APPOINTMENTS

J. Pulitzer, Jewish Editor and Publisher of the St. Louis Post-Dispatch, is reported as urging that the entire German General Staff, the industrialists and financiers, and almost all, if not all the members of the Gestapo and S. S. should be shot as war criminals.

The behind-the-scenes organizer of the International Military Tribunal to try "war criminals" is Judge Samuel I. Rosenman, Jewish adviser to the late President Roosevelt and to President Truman.

John J. O' Donnel, in his column Capitol Stuff, New York Daily News, 16th May 1946, writes:

"The job as chief prosecutor at the war crimes trial at Nurnberg was, of course, a carefully planned political build-up for (Justice Robert) Jackson, the candidate for Governor of New York. The record and legal philosophy developed at Nurnberg have utterly destroyed any standing that Jackson might have as an exponent of justice under law, but the boys still figure that the shabby performance can be transmuted into votes." (Evidently "the boys" changed their minds - it was too shabby.)

Allied Mission for German Reparations in Moscow has as its members:
American-Isador Lubin.
Polish - The Jewish Somerstajn.
British - The Jewish Sir David Waley
French - The Jewish Rueff.
Austrian Provisional Government:

The head of this government is Karl Renner ... On the 22nd June 1928 he wrote to President Masaryk of Czechoslovakia asking him to assist "in the interests of humanity" the escape of Bela Kun (known as Cohen, and leader of the red terror in Hungary and Spain) who was in Austria and wanted to go back to Russia. Renner said that he had enabled Kun to escape from Hungary to Russia on a former occasion (1919).

UNRRA-United Nations Relief and Rehabilitation Administration:
It's director-general was the Jewish Herbert Lehman. He was succeeded by Fiorello La Guardia of many Jewish connections. His wife is Jewish.

Their adopted children profess the Protestant faith.

Director General Lehman earlier in the year called British General Sir Frederick E. Morgan to New York to report on his statement of a well organized plan of the Jews, looking prosperous and well fed, to get out of Europe-a second exodus, he called it. Arriving in Berlin, with plenty of money, they certainly do not look like a persecuted people, he said. Mr. Lehman
exonerated General Morgan of any intent to belittle the plight of the Jews.

On August 21, 1946, the present Director General La Guardia is reported to have found it "possible to release General Morgan." He will be replaced by
Meyer Cohen.

UNRRA has many Jews on its staff: H. Alphand in France, in the Welfare Division is H. Greenstein; A. J. Rosemen was deputy chief in the Balkans; M. Gottschalk was a liaison officer in Frankfort. The UNRRA is not permitted to operate in Germany or Western Europe.

Mr. La Guardia made a VICIOUS attack on the Chicago Tribune when questioned about UNRRA funds.

UNO-United Nations Organization appointments:

Chairman of Committee to set up commission on control of Atomic Energy: The Jewish D. J. Manuilsky, Soviet Ukraine.

American member of the United Nations commission on Atomic Energy: Bernard Baruch. The Times (London) 19th March 1946 says "to him will be made over the results of the preliminary study of the problem of nuclear "fission," and David Lilienthal.

Assistant Secretary-General in charge of information is Benjamin Cohen.

American Representative on the Committee on UNRRA: Rep. Sol Bloom, also Chief of the Foreign Affairs Committee of the House of Representatives.

General Counsel to the Secretary-General: Abraham Feller.

Spanish Republican Government to replace Franco:

President: Diego Martinez Barrios, Grand Master of Spanish Grand Orient Freemasons.

Prime Minister: J. Giral, a Grand Orient Mason.

Foreign Secretary: The Jewish de los Rios.

Various National Appointments:

Ambassador Extraordinary for Economic and Financial Missions abroad for France: Leon Blum.

Charge d'Affaires for Poland in U. S. A. (Washington) : The Jewish Stephan Littauer (See Chapter I).

Consul General for Poland in U. S. A.; The Jewish J. Galewski.

Under-Secretary of State U. S. A.: Dean Acheson once the private secretary to Justice Louis D. Brandeis. He obtained his first important appointment through the influence of Justice Felix Frankfurter.

Official Observer in the Atom Bombing of Nagasaki: The Jewish journalist W. L. Lawrence.

French spokesman in Moscow re: plans for Ruhr and Rhineland: The Jewish H. Alphand.

Lord Chief Justice of Britain: Lord Goddard; his wife is a Jewess Schuster, Canadian Espionage Case, 1946:

The majority of the accused are Jewish. Fred Rose, the Communist M. P., whose real name is Rosenberg, and Sam Carr, whose real name is Cohen.

READ MARXISM AND JUDAISM, by Salluste.

A scholarly study of an important influence disturbing the peace of the world. A translation from the Revue de Paris. Price, 3 shillings.

Bibliography

A la Veille de la Renaissance, Eberlin.
American Hebrew.
American Journal of Semitic Languages.
Atlantic Monthly.
Carnegie Institute, Washington, D. C.
Case of Tyler Kent, John Howland Snow, Domestic and Foreign Affairs.
Century Magazine.
Chicago Tribune.
Cleveland News.
Coningsby, 1844.
Daily Express (London).
Daily Mail (London).
Daily Sketch (London).
Daily Telegraph (London).
Disgrace Abounding, Douglas Reed, Jonathan Cope.
Economist (London).
Evening News (London).
Evening Standard (London).
Financial News (London).
Financial (Times).
Foreign Capital in Poland, L. Wellicz.
Germany Must Perish, Theo Kaufman, Argyl Press, 1940.
Great Contemporaries, Winston Churchill.
Guerrilla Warfare.
Hand Book No. 43, Poland.
Hebrew Origins, J. T. Meek, Harpers, 1936.
Inside Story of the Peace Conference, E. J. Dillon, Harpers, 1920:
It Might Have Happened To You.
Jewish Chronicle (London)
Jewish Post
Jewish World.
La Revue de Paris.
La Vie de Tangier.

Leninism, Stalin.
Life (U. S. A)
Life of Arnold, Dean Staley.
Life of Lord George Bentinck.
London Times.
Manchester Guardian.
Marxism and Judaism, by Salluste, La Revue de Paris, Juillet Aout, 1928. First English translation. A scholarly study of an important influence disturbing the peace of the world. Price three shillings.
Masonic Chronicler, Waterloo, Wise., U. S. A.
New Leader (New York).
New York Daily News.
New York Journal - American.
New York Times.
Nineteenth Century.
A People's Runnymede, R. J. Scrutton, Andrew Dakers, 1924.
St. Louis Post-Dispatch.
Sunday Chronicle (London).
Sunday Express (London).
The Jews and Palestine, Samuel Landman.
The Jewish State, Theodor Herzl.
Toronto Evening Telegram.
Unfinished Victory, Arthur Bryant, Macmillan, 1940.
Washington Star.

www.ingramcontent.com/pod-product-compliance
Lightning Source LLC
Chambersburg PA
CBHW062111290426
44110CB00023B/2782